# AMERICAN CORPORATE IDENTITY 2002

### Edited by
## David E. Carter

**Cover Design**
**Jenette Williams**

**Book Design**
**Tania Lambert**

# American Corporate Identity 2002

First published 2001 by HBI,
an imprint of HarperCollins Publishers
10 East 53rd Street
New York, NY 10022-5299

ISBN:    0-06-018592-9

Distributed in the U.S. and Canada by
Watson-Guptill Publications
770 Broadway
New York, NY 10003-9595
Tel:      (800) 451-1741
            (732) 363-4511 in NJ, AK, HI
Fax:      (732) 363-0338

Distributed throughout the rest of the world by
HarperCollins International
10 East 53rd Street
New York, NY 10022-5299
Fax:       (212) 207-7654

Printed in Hong Kong by Everbest Printing Company through
Four Colour Imports, Louisville, Kentucky.

# Table of Contents

# COMPLETE
# CORPORATE
# IDENTITY
# PROGRAMS

CLIENT
  PeoplePC
DESIGN FIRM
  Landor Associates
DESIGNERS
  Patrick Cox, Fred Averin,
  Gaston Yagmourian
  Margaret Youngblood

# A Member of the France Telecom Group

CLIENT
  Global One
DESIGN FIRM
  Lister Butler Consulting
DESIGNERS
  John Lister, William Davis

A Member of the France Telecom Group

**Global Needs,
Global Solutions.**

GlobalOne.net

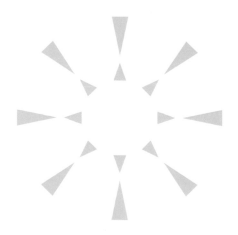

# SUMMITSTAGE

CLIENT
   Summit County, Colorado
DESIGN FIRM
   Noble Erickson Inc
DESIGNERS
   Jackie Noble, Steven Erickson,
   Robin Ridley

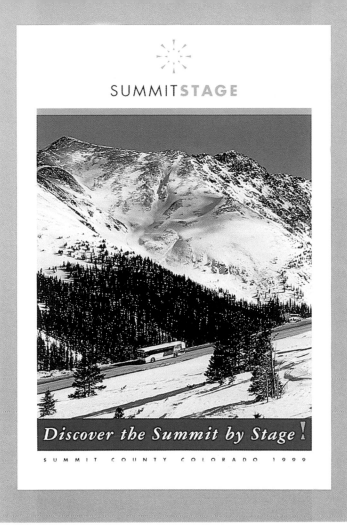

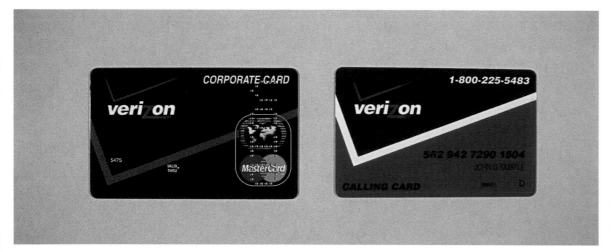

CLIENT
Verizon Communications
DESIGN FIRM
DeSola Group, Inc.
DESIGNERS
DeSola Group, Inc.

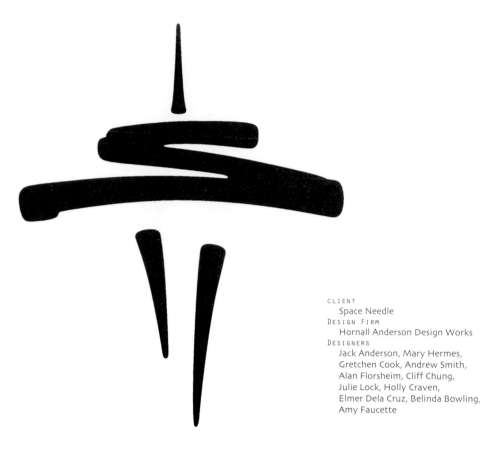

CLIENT
  Space Needle
DESIGN FIRM
  Hornall Anderson Design Works
DESIGNERS
  Jack Anderson, Mary Hermes,
  Gretchen Cook, Andrew Smith,
  Alan Florsheim, Cliff Chung,
  Julie Lock, Holly Craven,
  Elmer Dela Cruz, Belinda Bowling,
  Amy Faucette

# SoPbAaSsCeE

SKYLINE

DECK

skyCity

live the view

dinner

skyCity

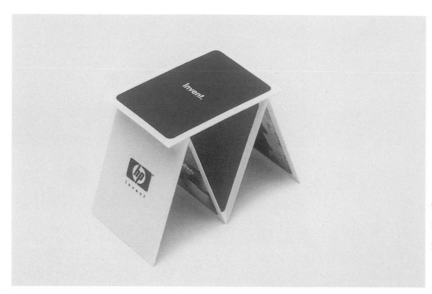

CLIENT
    Hewlett-Packard
DESIGN FIRM
    Landor Associates
DESIGNERS
    Margaret Youngblood, Patrick Cox,
    Frank Mueller, Paul Chock, Jean Loo,
    Christian Guler

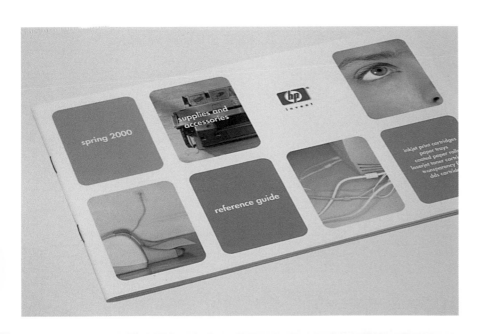

CLIENT
    Hot Commodities
DESIGN FIRM
    Koch Creative Services
DESIGNER
    Julie Lowrance

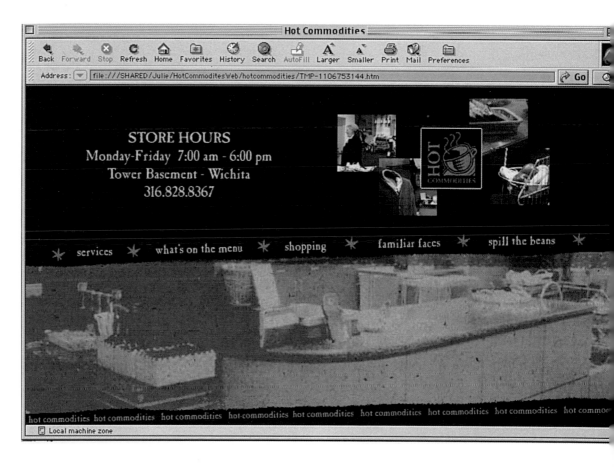

CLIENT
   Christie's
DESIGN FIRM
   Carbone Smolan Agency
DESIGNERS
   Claire Taylor, Koi Vatanapahu

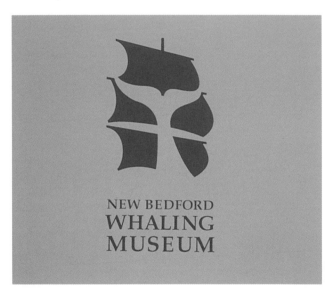

CLIENT
New Bedford Whaling Museum
DESIGN FIRM
Malcolm Grear Designers, Inc.

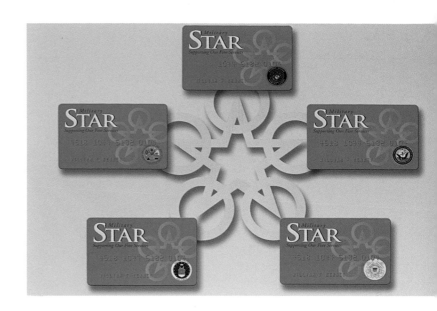

CLIENT
    Army Air Force Exchange Service
DESIGN FIRM
    BrandEquity International
DESIGNER
    Joe Selame

# bogart golf

CLIENT
Bogart Golf
DESIGN FIRM
Hornall Anderson Design Works
DESIGNERS
Jack Anderson, James Tee, Henry Yiu,
Holly Craven, Mary Hermes

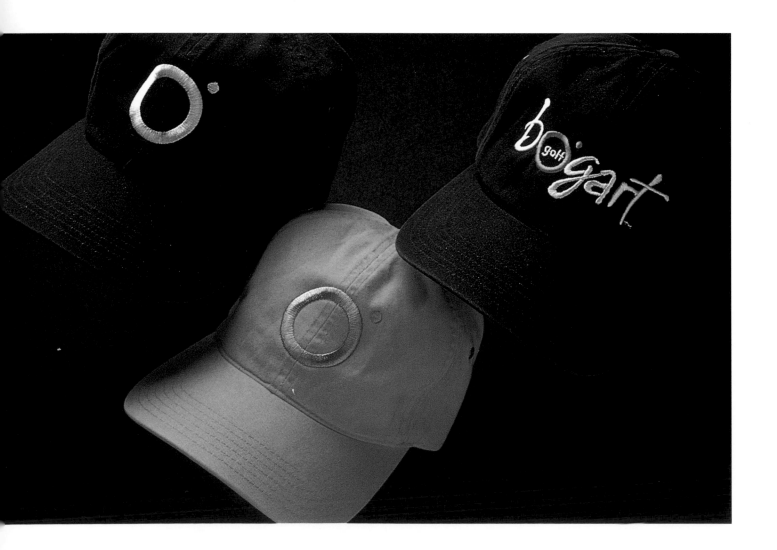

# Goodgrains

CLIENT
Goodgrains
DESIGN FIRM
FLUID
DESIGNERS
Blake DeJonge, Randi Trygstad

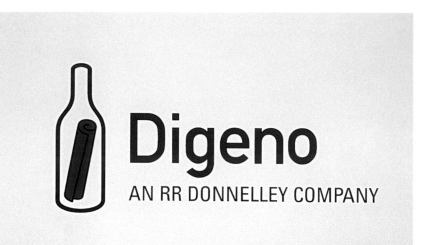

CLIENT
  RR Donnelly & Sons
DESIGN FIRM
  Landor Associates
DESIGNERS
  Margaret Youngblood, Matteo Vianello

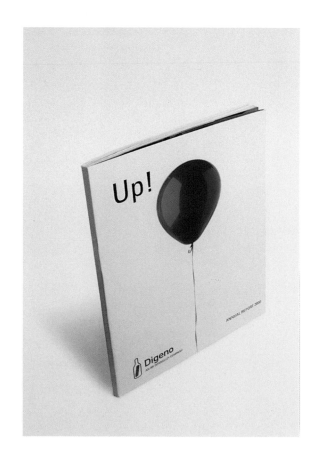

# HAYES
*design by nature*

CLIENT
The Hayes Company, Inc.
DESIGN FIRM
Insight Design Communications
DESIGNERS
Tracy Holdeman, Sherrie Holdeman

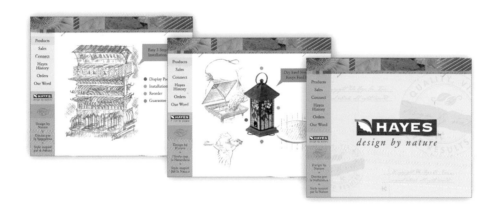

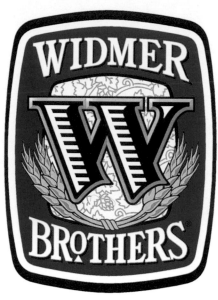

CLIENT
Widmer Brothers Brewery
DESIGN FIRM
Hornall Anderson Design Works
DESIGNERS
Jack Anderson, Larry Anderson, Bruce
Stigler, Bruce Branson-Meyer, Mary
Chin Hutchison, Michael Brugman,
Ed Lee, Kaye Farmer

# MULVANNY

## ARCHITECTS

CLIENT
  Mulvanny Architects
DESIGN FIRM
  Walsh & Associates, Inc.
DESIGNERS
  Miriam Lisco, Lyn Blanchard,
  Rob West

# SAKSON & TAYLOR

CLIENT
  Sakson & Taylor
DESIGN FIRM
  Walsh & Associates, Inc.
DESIGNERS
  Miriam Lisco, Rob West

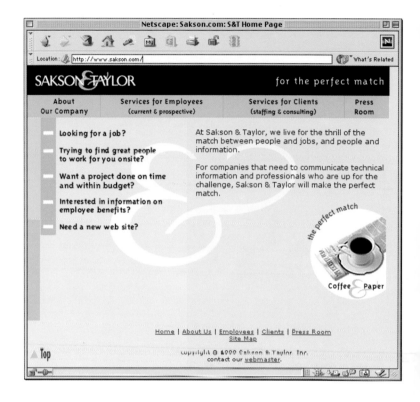

S&T OnSite

A DIVISION OF SAKSON & TAYLOR, INC.

S&T Consulting

A DIVISION OF SAKSON & TAYLOR, INC.

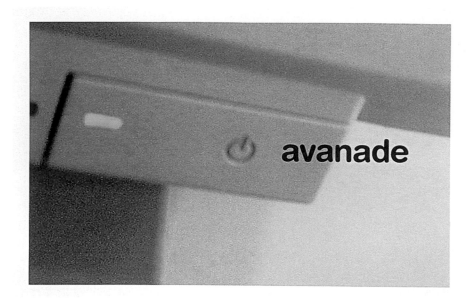

CLIENT
  Avanade
DESIGN FIRM
  Landor Associates
DESIGNERS
  Gail Taras, Alessio Krauss
  Margaret Youngblood

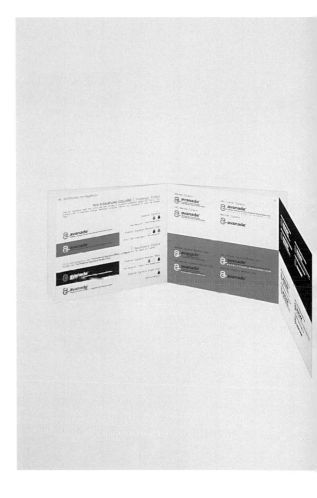

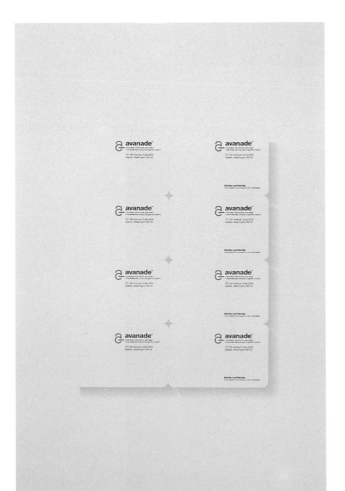

CLIENT
RPM
DESIGN FIRM
Hornall Anderson Design Works
DESIGNERS
Jack Anderson, Kathy Saito,
Alan Copeland, Sonja Max,
Cliff Chung

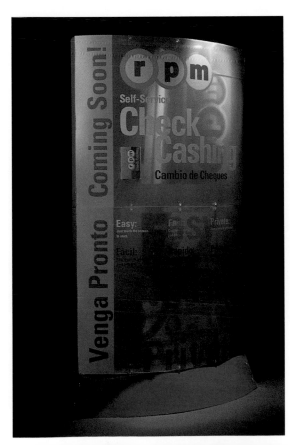

H&R BLOCK®

CLIENT
    H&R Block
DESIGN FIRM
    Landor Associates
DESIGNERS
    Margaret Youngblood, Eric Scott,
    Kisitina Wong, Tina Schoepflin,
    Irena Block, David Rockwell,
    Mary Hayano, Cameron Imani

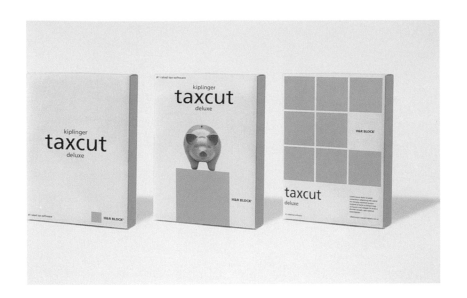

CLIENT
    The Cleveland Indians
DESIGN FIRM
    Herip Associates
DESIGNERS
    Walter M. Herip, John R. Menter

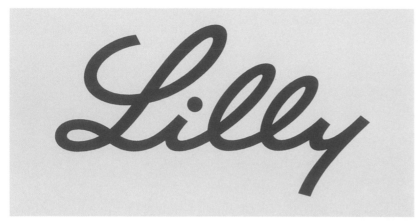

CLIENT
  Eli Lilly & Company
DESIGN FIRM
  Landor Associates
DESIGNERS
  Margaret Youngblood
  Margo Zucker, Thomas Bossert,
  Frank Mueller, Michele Berry,
  Pia Carino, John Bowers,
  Brad Scott, Rebecca Titcomb

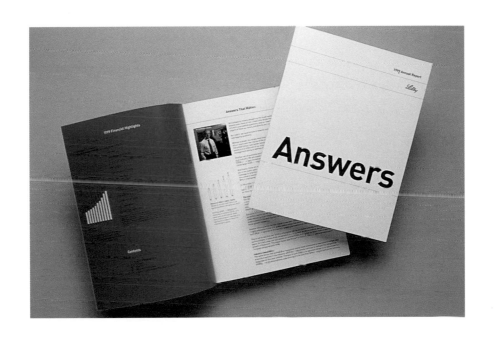

# 25 YEARS Cuyahoga Valley
## National Recreation Area

CLIENT
Cuyahoga Valley National Park
DESIGN FIRM
Herip Associates
DESIGNERS
Walter M. Herip, John R. Menter

# PACKAGE
# DESIGN

CLIENT
   Domino's Pizza
DESIGN FIRM
   Addison
DESIGNERS
   Nick Bentley, Kraig Kessel

CLIENT
   The Quaker Oats Company
DESIGN FIRM
   Haugaard Creative Group, Inc.
DESIGNER
   Jose Parado

CLIENT
   The Wine Group
DESIGN FIRM
   Enterprise/IG
DESIGNER
   Richard Patterson

CLIENT
   The Coca-Cola Company
DESIGN FIRM
   Lipson Alport Glass & Assoc.
DESIGNERS
   Jon Shapiro, Lori Cerwin,
   Tracy Bacilek

CLIENT
   United Parcel Service of America, Inc.
DESIGN FIRM
   Wages Design
DESIGNERS
   Joanna Tak, Matt Taylor

CLIENT
   Procter & Gamble
DESIGN FIRM
   Lipson Alport Glass & Assoc.
DESIGNERS
   Mike Skrzelowski, Gary Sample

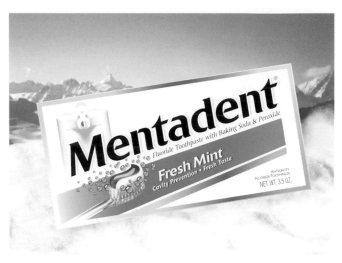

CLIENT
Welch's
DESIGN FIRM
Bailey Design Group
DESIGNERS
Dave Fiedler, Steve Perry,
Amy Anstine, Layne Lyons

CLIENT
Unilever HPC, USA
DESIGN FIRM
Hans Flink Design Inc.
DESIGNERS
Chang-Mei Lin

CLIENT
Sony Electronics, Inc.
DESIGN FIRM
Sony Design Center
DESIGNER
Rosaline Yin

CLIENT
Nestle USA, Inc.
DESIGN FIRM
Thompson Design Group
DESIGNERS
Tony Albright, Patrick Fraser,
Dan Bishop, Dennis Thompson

CLIENT
Guittard Chocolates
DESIGN FIRM
Hornall Anderson Design Works
DESIGNERS
Jana Nishi, Debra McCloskey,
Margaret Long, Belinda Bowling

CLIENT
Patti's Pickledilly Pickles
DESIGN FIRM
Mark Oliver, Inc.
DESIGNERS
Mark Oliver, Patty Driskel

CLIENT
Jacob Leinenkugel Brewing Company
DESIGN FIRM
Design Partners Incorporated
DESIGNERS
Sally Brown

CLIENT
The Gillette Co.
DESIGN FIRM
Phillips Design Group
DESIGNERS
Alison Goudreault, Glenn Soulia

CLIENT
Wallace Church, Inc.
DESIGN FIRM
Wallace Church, Inc.
DESIGNERS
Stan Church, David Minkley,
Wendy Church

CLIENT
World Kitchen
DESIGN FIRM
Interbrand Hulefeld
DESIGNER
Christian Neidhard

CLIENT
Sara Lee Underwear
DESIGN FIRM
Lipson Alport Glass & Assoc.
DESIGNERS
Ryan Green, Jon Shapiro

CLIENT
Kraft Foods, Inc.
DESIGN FIRM
Design Partners
Incorporated
DESIGNER
Barbara Hannagan

CLIENT
Target Packaging
DESIGN FIRM
Franke
DESIGNER
Jill Barklem

CLIENT
H.P. Hood, Inc.
DESIGN FIRM
Hughes Design Group/
Hood Design Group
DESIGNERS
K. Leunis, C. Giordano

CLIENT
Stolpman Vineyards
DESIGN FIRM
Axioin Design Inc.

CLIENT
neu, inc.
DESIGN FIRM
Design Guys
DESIGNERS
Steven Sikora,
Jerry Stenback

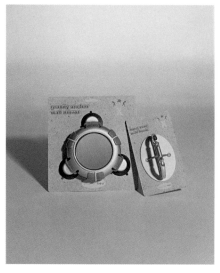

CLIENT
Bellwether Farms
DESIGN FIRM
Mark Oliver, Inc.
DESIGNERS
Mark Oliver, Patty Devlin-Driskel

CLIENT
Target Packaging
DESIGN FIRM
Target Softlines
DESIGNER
Ron Anderson

CLIENT
Sugar Beats
DESIGNER
Todd Nickel

CLIENT
Printing Inc.
DESIGN FIRM
LPG Design
DESIGNERS
Rick Gimlin, Dustin Commer,
Lorna West, Chris West

CLIENT
Meijer Inc.
DESIGN FIRM
Interbrand Hulefeld
DESIGNERS
Dennis Dill, Rick Murphy,
Jose Luis Calderon-Parada

CLIENT
Imagine Foods
DESIGN FIRM
Gauger & Silva
DESIGNER
Isabelle LaPorte

CLIENT
Target Packaging
DESIGN FIRM
Target
DESIGNER
Brad Hartman

CLIENT
Time Life Video
DESIGN FIRM
WorkHorse Creative
DESIGNER
David Vogin

CLIENT
Turkey Hill Dairy
DESIGN FIRM
Wallace Church, Inc.
DESIGNERS
Stan Church, Nin Glaister,
David Minkley

CLIENT
Calio Groves
DESIGN FIRM
Axion Design Inc.

CLIENT
Telestar Interactive Corporation
DESIGN FIRM
Visual Marketing Associates, Inc.
DESIGNERS
Kenneth Botts, Tracy Meiners

CLIENT
Max & Lucy
DESIGN FIRM
After Hours Creative
DESIGNERS
After Hours Creative

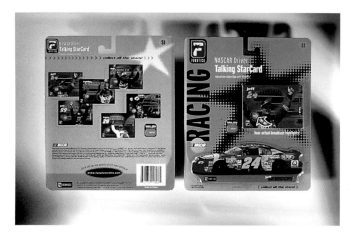

CLIENT
Mott's North America
DESIGN FIRM
Zunda Design Group
DESIGNERS
Charles Zunda,
Patrick Sullivan

CLIENT
Johnson & Johnson
DESIGN FIRM
Baily Design Group
DESIGNERS
Dave Fiedler, Steve Perry,
Denise Bosler

CLIENT
Nissley Vineyards
DESIGN FIRM
Albert/Bogner Design
DESIGNER
Marie-Elaina Miller

CLIENT
Blistex, Inc.
DESIGN FIRM
Di Donato Associates
DESIGNER
Don Childs

CLIENT
Target Stores
DESIGN FIRM
Design Guys
DESIGNERS
Steven Sikora,
Gary Patch

CLIENT
Tokyo Bay
DESIGN FIRM
Levin Breidenbach Wade
DESIGNERS
Stephanie Wade, Jeff Breidenbach

CLIENT
Loft
DESIGN FIRM
Mastandrea Design, Inc.
DESIGNER
Mary Anne Mastandrea

CLIENT
The Quaker Oats Company
DESIGN FIRM
Haugaard Creative Group
DESIGNER
Jose Parado

CLIENT
    Kids II, Inc.
DESIGN FIRM
    Wages Design
DESIGNERS
    Dominga Lee, Matt Taylor

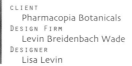

CLIENT
    Pharmacopia Botanicals
DESIGN FIRM
    Levin Breidenbach Wade
DESIGNER
    Lisa Levin

CLIENT
    Le Petit Chef
DESIGN FIRM
    Insight Design Communications
DESIGNERS
    Tracy Holdeman,
    Sherrie Holdeman

CLIENT
    Kemps/Marigold
DESIGN FIRM
    Compass Design
DESIGNERS
    Mitchell Lindgren,
    Tom Arthur, Rich McGowen

CLIENT
    Anheuser-Busch
DESIGN FIRM
    Deutsch Design Works
DESIGNERS
    John Marota, Barry Deutsch, Gregg Perin

CLIENT
    Chuppa Chups U.S.A.
DESIGN FIRM
    Zunda Design Group
DESIGNER
    Todd Nickel

CLIENT
Time Life Music
DESIGN FIRM
WorkHorse Creative
DESIGNERS
David Vogin, James Hersick

CLIENT
Cougar Mountain Bakery
DESIGN FIRM
Hornall Anderson Design Works
DESIGNERS
Jack Anderson, Debra McCloskey, Lisa Cerveny, Holly Craven,
Mary Chin Hutchison, Gretchen Cook, Morothee Soechting

CLIENT
William Grant & Sons
DESIGN FIRM
Bailey Design Group
DESIGNERS
Steve Perry, Wendy Slavish,
Christian Williamson

CLIENT
Breeder's Choice
DESIGN FIRM
Mark Oliver, Inc.
DESIGNERS
Mark Oliver, Patty Driskel

CLIENT
Dental Concepts
DESIGN FIRM
Handler Design Group, Inc.
DESIGNER
Bruce Handler

CLIENT
Archway-Mother's Cookies
DESIGN FIRM
Axion Design Inc.

CLIENT
   Mark Anthony Brands
DESIGN FIRM
   Mastandrea Design, Inc.
DESIGNER
   Mary Anne Mastandrea

CLIENT
   Burning Hole LLC.
DESIGN FIRM
   Meteor Marketing
DESIGNER
   Max Maxwell

CLIENT
   Kroger Company
DESIGN FIRM
   Interbrand Hulefeld
DESIGNER
   Christian Neidhard

CLIENT
   United Distillers & Vintners
DESIGN FIRM
   Port Miolla Design
DESIGNER
   Ralph J. Miolla

CLIENT
Stewarts Beverages
DESIGN FIRM
Rassman Design
DESIGNERS
John Rassman, Lyn D'Amato

CLIENT
Marsh Inc.
DESIGN FIRM
Interbrand Hulefeld
DESIGNERS
Rick Murphy, Les Maass

CLIENT
Target Stores
DESIGN FIRM
Hedstrom/Blessing, Inc.
DESIGNER
Wendy LaBreche

CLIENT
Wallace Church, Inc.
DESIGN FIRM
Wallace Church, Inc.
DESIGNERS
Nereida Lopez, Stan Church

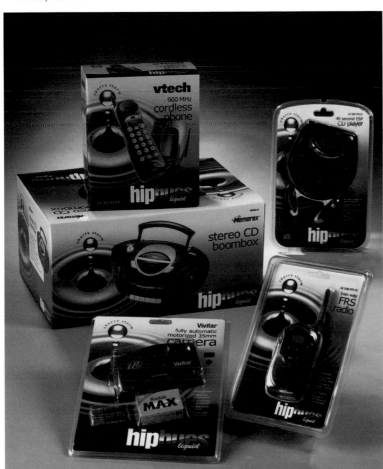

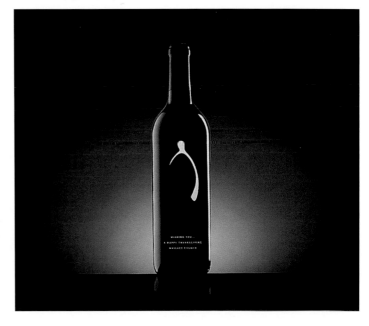

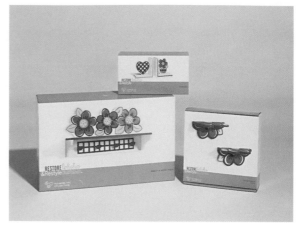

CLIENT
Doughmakers, LLC.
DESIGN FIRM
Miller & White Advertising, Inc.
DESIGNER
Jenny Hoffeditz

CLIENT
Target Stores
DESIGN FIRM
Design Guys
DESIGNERS
Steven Sikora,
Jerry Stenback, Gary Patch

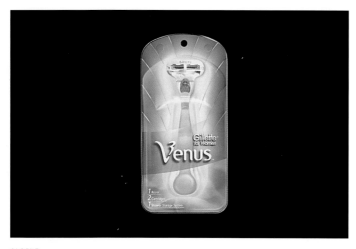

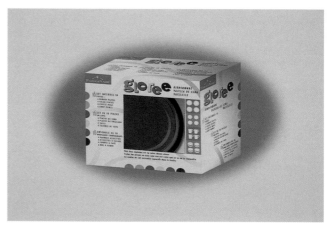

CLIENT
Gillette Co.
DESIGN FIRM
Wallach Church, Inc.
DESIGNERS
Lawrence Haggerty, John Bruno,
Stan Church

CLIENT
Continuum Sales & Marketing Corp.
DESIGN FIRM
Gold Forest
DESIGNERS
Peter Blandori, Ray Garcia,
Michael Gold, Lauren Gold

CLIENT
The Gillette Company
DESIGN FIRM
Phillips Design Group
DESIGNER
Alison Goudreault

CLIENT
Target Packaging
DESIGN FIRM
One Buck Design
DESIGNERS
One Buck Design

CLIENT
    Kemps/Marigold
DESIGN FIRM
    Compass Design
DESIGNERS
    Mitchell Lindgren,
    Tom Arthur, Rich McGowen

CLIENT
    Actron
DESIGN FIRM
    Deskey
DESIGNER
    Anouk Shofield

CLIENT
    Phil Goode Grocery
DESIGN FIRM
    Sayles Graphic Design
DESIGNER
    John Sayles

CLIENT
    Beringer Wine Estates
DESIGN FIRM
    Enterprise/IG
DESIGNER
    Thomas Harley Bond

CLIENT
    Farmland Industries, Inc.
DESIGN FIRM
    Lipson Alport Glass & Assoc.
DESIGNERS
    Phil Weintraub, Ryan Green

CLIENT
    North Aire Foods
DESIGN FIRM
    Compass Design
DESIGNERS
    Mitchell Lindgren,
    Tom Arthur, Rich McGowen

CLIENT
Kemps/Marigold
DESIGN FIRM
Compass Design
DESIGNERS
Mitchell Lindgren,
Tom Arthur, Rich McGowen

CLIENT
Personal Health Development
DESIGN FIRM
Jensen Design Assoc. Inc.
DESIGNERS
David Jensen, Andre Gomez,
Stephanie Hall, Jerome Calleja

CLIENT
United Distillers & Vintners
DESIGN FIRM
Port Miolla Design
DESIGNERS
Paul A. Port, Ralph J. Miolla,
Jeffrey Meyer

CLIENT
Miller Brewing Company
DESIGN FIRM
Design Partners Incorporated
DESIGNER
Jim Jedlicka

CLIENT
Target Packaging
DESIGN FIRM
Target Softlines
DESIGNER
Angela Johansen

CLIENT
American Dairy Co.
DESIGN FIRM
Enterprise/IG
DESIGNER
Richard Patterson

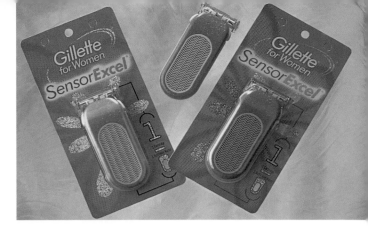

CLIENT
The Gillette Company
DESIGN FIRM
Phillips Design Group
DESIGNER
Susan Logcher

CLIENT
Dental Concepts
DESIGN FIRM
Handler Design Group, Inc.
DESIGNER
Bruce Handler

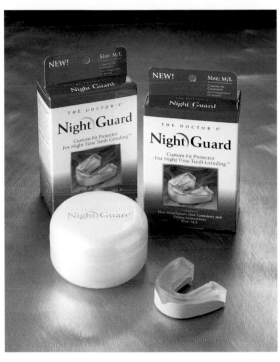

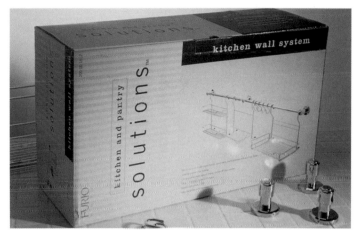

CLIENT
Dental Concepts
DESIGN FIRM
Handler Design Group, Inc
DESIGNER
Bruce Handler

CLIENT
Target Packaging
DESIGN FIRM
Target Advertising
DESIGNER
Jason Langer

CLIENT
Target Packaging
DESIGN FIRM
Target Packaging
DESIGNER
Molly Davis

CLIENT
Target Packaging
DESIGN FIRM
Design Guys, Mlps, MN
DESIGNER
Sandra Fazio

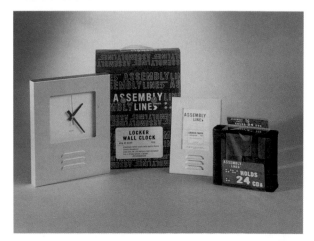

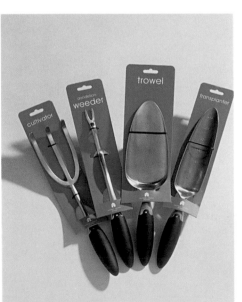

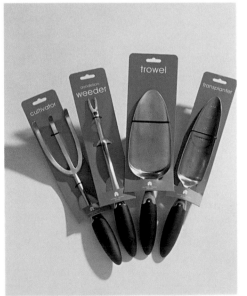

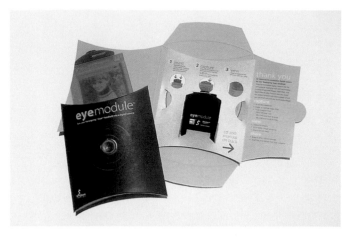

CLIENT
IDEO
DESIGN FIRM
1185 Design
DESIGNERS
Peggy Burke, Millie Hsi,
Merry Biggerstaff

CLIENT
United Distillers + Vintners
DESIGN FIRM
Axion Design Inc.

CLIENT
Taylor Made Golf Co.
DESIGN FIRM
Laura Coe Design Assoc
DESIGNERS
Leanne Leveillee, Jenny Goddard,
Tom Richman, Laura Coe Wright,
Ryolchl Yotsumoto

CLIENT
Target Stores
DESIGN FIRM
Design Guys
DESIGNERS
Steven Sikora, Jerry Stenback

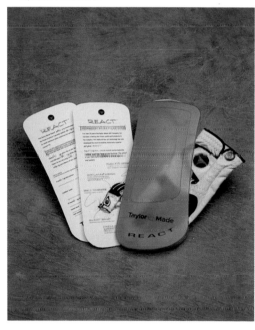

CLIENT
Samsung
DESIGN FIRM
Handler Design Group, Inc.
DESIGNERS
Bruce Handler, Leah Kent

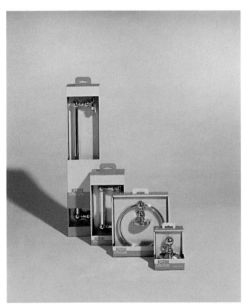

CLIENT
Target Stores
DESIGN FIRM
Design Guys
DESIGNER
Steven Sikora,
Nancy Blackwell Bolan

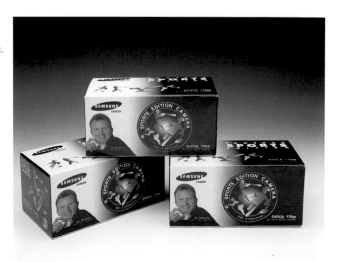

CLIENT
M&M Mars
DESIGN FIRM
Wallace Church, Inc.
DESIGNERS
John Bruno, Stan Church

CLIENT
Drinks That Work
DESIGN FIRM
Enterprise/IG
DESIGNER
Amy Hershman

CLIENT
Snapple Beverage Group
DESIGN FIRM
HMS Design, Inc.

CLIENT
William Grant & Sons
DESIGN FIRM
Bailey Design Group
DESIGNERS
Steve Perry, Kelly Beh

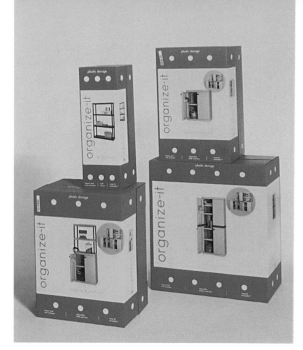

CLIENT
  Time Life Video
DESIGN FIRM
  WorkHorse Creative
DESIGNERS
  David Vogin, Lesley Quesada

CLIENT
  Target Stores
DESIGN FIRM
  Design Guys
DESIGNER
  Steven Sikora, John Moes

CLIENT
  Seagram Beverage Company
DESIGN FIRM
  Port Miolla Design
DESIGNER
  Jeffrey Meyer

CLIENT
  Sony Trans Com, Inc.
DESIGN FIRM
  Nostrum Advertising, Inc.
DESIGNERS
  Joanna Lee, Michelle DonVito

CLIENT
M
DESIGN FIRM
Supon Design Group
DESIGNERS
Supon Phornirunlit,
Tom Klinedinst

CLIENT
Target Stores
DESIGN FIRM
Design Guys
DESIGNERS
Steven Sikora, Jerry Stenback,
Gary Patch

CLIENT
Paris Las Vegas-Teresa Malm
DESIGN FIRM
Ripple Strategic
Design & Consulting
DESIGNERS
Dan McElhattan III,
Raymond Perez, Laura Zollar

CLIENT
United Distillers & Vintners
DESIGN FIRM
Port Miolla Design
DESIGNERS
Port Miolla Associates

CLIENT
Kemps/Marigold
DESIGN FIRM
Compass Design
DESIGNERS
Mitchell Lindgren, Tom Arthur,
Rich McGowen

CLIENT
Actron
DESIGN FIRM
Deskey
DESIGNERS
Genie King, Claudio Octaviano

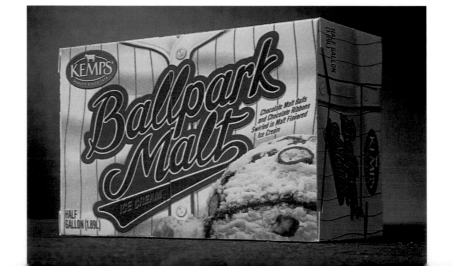

CLIENT
CreAgri, LLC
DESIGN FIRM
Mastandrea Design, Inc.
DESIGNER
Mary Anne Mastandrea

CLIENT
Compago Creative
DESIGN FIRM
Compago Creative
DESIGNER
Sandra Pirie-St. Amour

CLIENT
totes/Isotoner
DESIGN FIRM
Visual Marketing
Associates, Inc.
DESIGNERS
Amy Baas, Julie Haws,
Tracy Meiners

CLIENT
Chieftain Wild Rice
DESIGN FIRM
Compass Design
DESIGNERS
Mitchell Lindgren, Tom Arthur,
Rich McGowen, Sharon Sudman

CLIENT
Allied Domecq
DESIGN FIRM
Enterprise/IG
DESIGNER
Thomas Harley Bond

CLIENT
B + G Foods, Inc.
DESIGN FIRM
Zunda Design Group
DESIGNERS
Charles Zunda, Todd Nickel,
Patrick Sullivan

CLIENT
  Time Life Video
DESIGN FIRM
  WorkHorse Creative
DESIGNERS
  David Vogin, James Hersick

CLIENT
  Bartolomeh
DESIGN FIRM
  Culinane Design
DESIGNER
  Carmen Li

CLIENT
  Meijer Inc.
DESIGN FIRM
  Interbrand Hulefeld
DESIGNERS
  Rick Murphy,
   Jose Luis Calderon-Parada

CLIENT
  Meijer Inc.
DESIGN FIRM
  Interbrand Hulefeld
DESIGNERS
  Rick Murphy,
   Jose Luis Calderon-Parada

CLIENT
 Kemps/Marigold
DESIGN FIRM
 Compass Design
DESIGNERS
 Mitchell Lindgren,
 Tom Arthur, Rich McGowen

CLIENT
 Pamela's Products
DESIGN FIRM
 Dickson Design
DESIGNER
 Deborah Shea

CLIENT
 Perdue Farms
DESIGN FIRM
 Harbauer Bruce Nelson
DESIGNERS
 Steve Walker, Eric Williams

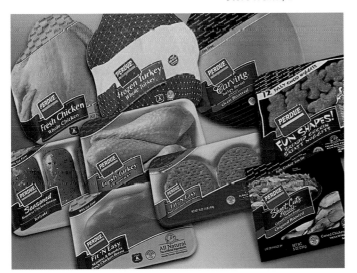

CLIENT
 Tear Of The Clouds, LLC
DESIGN FIRM
 Zunda Design Group
DESIGNERS
 Todd Nickel, Charles Zunda

CLIENT
Westwood Studios
DESIGN FIRM
Creative Dynamics, Inc.
DESIGNERS
Eddie Roberts, Casey Corcoran,
Victoria Hart

CLIENT
Time Life Video
DESIGN FIRM
WorkHorse Creative
DESIGNER
David Vogin

CLIENT
Canandaigua Wine Company
DESIGN FIRM
Forward Branding & Identity
DESIGNER
Brenda Benedict

CLIENT
Target Packaging
DESIGN FIRM
WorkHorse Studio
DESIGNER
Sandra Fazio

CLIENT
United Distillers
& Vintners
DESIGN FIRM
Port Miolla Design
DESIGNERS
David Matthai,
Ralph J. Miolla

CLIENT
Wegmans
DESIGN FIRM
Forward Branding & Identity
DESIGNER
Wendy Foster

CLIENT
  Target Packaging
DESIGN FIRM
  Target Packaging
DESIGNER
  Molly Davis

CLIENT
  The Hayes Company, Inc.
DESIGN FIRM
  Insight Design Communications
DESIGNER
  Tracy Holdeman, Sherrie Holdeman

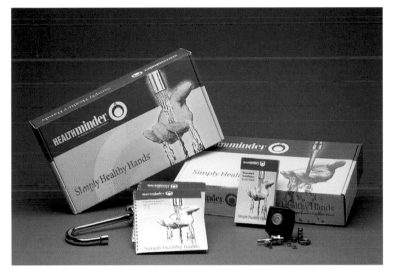

CLIENT
  Healthminder
DESIGN FIRM
  Baer Design Group
DESIGNER
  Todd Baer

CLIENT
  Procter & Gamble
DESIGN FIRM
  Interbrand Hulefeld
DESIGNER
  Christian Neidhard

CLIENT
  Taylor Made Golf Co.
DESIGN FIRM
  Laura Coe Design Assoc.
DESIGNERS
  Ryoichi Yotsumoto,
  Laura Coe Wright

CLIENT
  Ingersoll-Rand
DESIGN FIRM
  Deskey
DESIGNERS
  Claudio Octaviano, Genie King

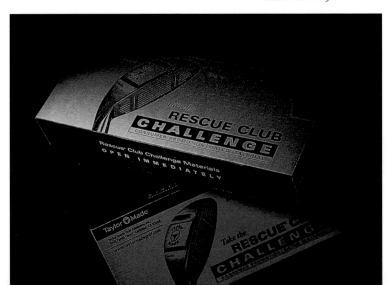

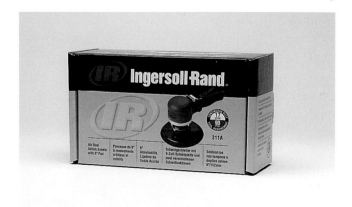

CLIENT
  Wegmans Food Markets
DESIGN FIRM
  Icon Graphics, Inc.
DESIGNERS
  Icon Graphics, Inc.

CLIENT
  Peet's Coffee & Tea
DESIGN FIRM
  Enterprise/IG
DESIGNERS
  Phillip Ting, Carrie Binney

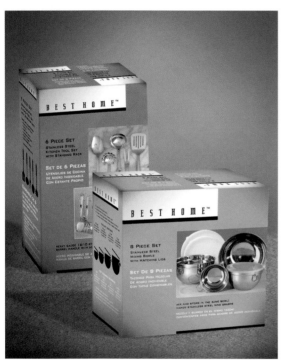

CLIENT
  Continuum Sales &
  Marketing Corp.
DESIGN FIRM
  Gold Forest
DESIGNERS
  Peter Blandori, Ray Garcia,
  Michael Gold, Lauren Gold

CLIENT
  Mixology
DESIGN FIRM
  DeSola Group, Inc.
DESIGNERS
  DeSola Group, Inc.

CLIENT
  Anheuser-Busch
DESIGN FIRM
  Deutsch Design Works
DESIGNERS
  John Marota, Barry Deutsch,
  Gregg Perin

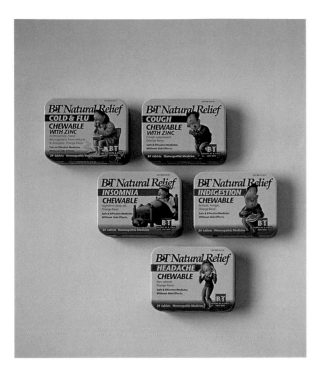

CLIENT
   Boericke & Tafel
DESIGN FIRM
   Gauger & Silva
DESIGNER
   Bob Ankers

CLIENT
   Robert Mondavi Winery
DESIGN FIRM
   Deutsch Design Works
DESIGNERS
   Mark Dolin, Barry Deutsch,
   Dexter Lee, Jacques Rossouw

CLIENT
   Target Stores
DESIGN FIRM
   Design Guys
DESIGNERS
   Steven Sikora, Dawn Selg

CLIENT
   Guinness Bass Import Co.
DESIGN FIRM
   Axion Design Inc.

CLIENT
As We Change
DESIGN FIRM
Laura Coe Design Assoc.
DESIGNERS
Tracy Castle, Ryoichi Yotsumoto,
Laura Coe Wright

CLIENT
Robert Mondavi Winery
DESIGN FIRM
Deutsch Design Works
DESIGNERS
Mark Dolin, Barry Deutsch,
Jacques Rossouw

CLIENT
Kemps/Marigold
DESIGN FIRM
Compass Design
DESIGNERS
Mitchell Lindgren, Tom Arthur,
Rich McGowen, Bill Collins

CLIENT
Kemps/Marigold
DESIGN FIRM
Compass Design
DESIGNERS
Mitchell Lindgren, Tom Arthur,
Rich McGowen, Sharon Sudman

CLIENT
Target Packaging
DESIGN FIRM
Fame, Minneapolis, MN
DESIGNERS
Fame

# LETTERHEAD DESIGNS

# CLEAN & POLISH

966 HUNGERFORD DRIVE, SUITE 18A
ROCKVILLE, MD 20850
T 301.424.1516  800.811.4989
F 301.424.7415
WWW.CLEANANDPOLISH.COM

CLIENT
    Clean & Polish, Inc.
DESIGN FIRM
    Supon Design Group
DESIGNERS
    Supon Phornirunlit,
    Pum Mek-Aroonreung

CLIENT
    Spokane Parks Foundation
DESIGN FIRM
    Klundt Hosmer Design
DESIGNERS
    Amy Gunter, Darin Klundt

SPOKANE PARKS FOUNDATION

808 W. SPOKANE FALLS BLVD.
SPOKANE, WASHINGTON 99201

(509)625-6774 · FAX (509)625-6205
www.spokanecity.org/parks/foundation

CLIENT
   DPI-Digital Prepress
   International
DESIGN FIRM
   Oh Boy, A Design Company
DESIGNERS
   Ted Bluey, David Salanitro

**DPi**
Digital Prepress International

645 Mariposa Street
San Francisco, CA 94107

t  415 882 9961
f  415 882 9977

01 Prepress
02 Digital Photography
03 Digital Printing

04 Retouching
05 Display Graphics
06 Offset Lithography

07 Book Manufacturing
08 Fine Art Reproduction
09 Versatility

www.apartmentzero.com

apartment**zero**

406 7th street, nw
washington, dc 20004
t. 202.628.4067
f. 202.628.4069

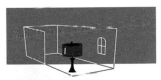

apartment**zero**

406 7th street, nw
washington, dc 20004

CHRISTOPHER RALGTON

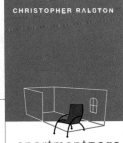

apartment**zero**

406 7th street, nw
washington, dc 20004
t. 202.628.4067
f. 202.628.4069
www.apartmentzero.com

CLIENT
   Apartment Zero
DESIGN FIRM
   Supon Design Group
DESIGNERS
   Supon Phornirunlit,
   Pum Mek-Aroonreung

# circles
**mission accomplished**

300 Congress Street    **T** 617.622.6200
Boston, MA 02210    **F** 617.622.6220
**www.circles.com**

CLIENT
Circles
DESIGN FIRM
Corey McPherson Nash
DESIGNERS
Michael McPherson, Rich Rose

# LIQUID2REALITY

80 FIFTH AVENUE, SUITE 708, NEW YORK, NY 10011   t: 212.924.3400   f: 212.924.0556

www.LIQUID2REALITY.com

**CRAIG ROSENMAN**
PRESIDENT

# L2R

LIQUID2REALITY DESIGN
80 FIFTH AVENUE, SUITE 708
NEW YORK, NY 10011
t: 212.924.3400   f: 212.924.2556
CRAIG@LIQUID2REALITY.COM

CLIENT
Liquid2reality, Inc.
DESIGN FIRM
Liquid2reality, Inc.
DESIGNERS
Carlos Gonzalez

## Seattle Architectural Foundation

CLIENT
Seattle Architectural Foundation
DESIGN FIRM
Michael Courtney Design
DESIGNERS
Mike Courtney, Scott Souchock,
Dan Hoang

CLIENT
Coturn Gigs
DESIGN FIRM
über, Inc.
DESIGNERS
Jimmy Ng, David Wolf

CLIENT
Infinite Functions
DESIGN FIRM
Cintara Corporation
DESIGNER
Qui Tong

INFINITE
FUNCTIONS

1660 Hamilton Ave.  |  Suite 205  |  San Jose, CA  |  95125  |  p: 408.445.7480  |  f: 408.445.7481

Infinite Functions, Inc.

www.infinitefunctions.com

TOMPERTDESIGN
LOGO DESIGN & WEBSITE DEVELOPMENT

‹TOMPERTDESIGN›
‹NAME›**Claudia Huber Tompert**
‹STREET›216 Fulton Street
‹CITY›Palo Alto
‹STATE›California
‹ZIP›94301
‹PHONE›650.323.0365
‹EMAIL›claudia@tompert.com
‹WEBSITE›www.tompertdesign.com
‹FAX›650.323.0366
‹/TOMPERTDESIGN›

TOMPERTDESIGN
LOGO DESIGN & WEBSITE DEVELOPMENT

CLIENT
tompertdesign
DESIGN FIRM
tompertdesign
DESIGNERS
Claudia Huber Tompert,
Michael Tompert

‹STREET›216 Fulton Street
‹CITY›Palo Alto
‹STATE_ZIP›California 94301
‹PHONE›650.323.0365
‹EMAIL›mail@tompert.com
‹WEBSITE›www.tompertdesign.com
‹FAX›650.323.0366

CLIENT
Oryx Executive Search
DESIGN FIRM
Melissa Passehl Design
DESIGNERS
Melissa Passehl, Desiree Jue

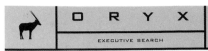

ORYX

EXECUTIVE SEARCH

3235 KIFER ROAD, SUITE 340
SANTA CLARA, CALIFORNIA 95051

TEL 408.481.0100
FAX 408.481.0123

WWW.ORYXSEARCH.COM

BOTANICUS

7610-T Rickenbacker Drive, Gaithersburg, MD 20879

email: botanicus@erols.com   301.977.8887   1.800.282.8887   fax: 301.330.9287

BOTANICUS

7610-T Rickenbacker Drive
Gaithersburg, MD 20879

BOTANICUS

SCOTT
SILBERMAN

7610-T Rickenbacker Drive
Gaithersburg, MD 20879
email: botanicus@erols.com
301.977.8887
1.800.282.8887
fax: 301.330.9287

the EVOLUTION of FRAGRANCE

CLIENT
Botanicus
DESIGN FIRM
Gibson Creative
DESIGNERS
Kelly Bush, Juliette Brown

CLIENT
West + Associates
DESIGN FIRM
West + Associates
DESIGNERS
Brian Rush, Shane Kendrick

W—ST

WEST+ASSOCIATES, INC.
MARKETING | DESIGN

1420 spring hill road
suite 325
mclean, va | 22102

Beaulieu Vineyard.
SINCE 1900
BV

BEAULIEU VINEYARD

1960 ST HELENA HWY

POST OFFICE BOX 219

RUTHERFORD, CA 94573

TEL 707 967 5200

FAX 707 963 5920

WWW.BVWINE.COM

| P. | 703.893.0404 |
| F. | 703.893.0988 |
| W. | WESTASSOC1.COM |

CLIENT
Beaulieu Vineyard
DESIGN FIRM
Halleck
DESIGNER
Wayne Wright

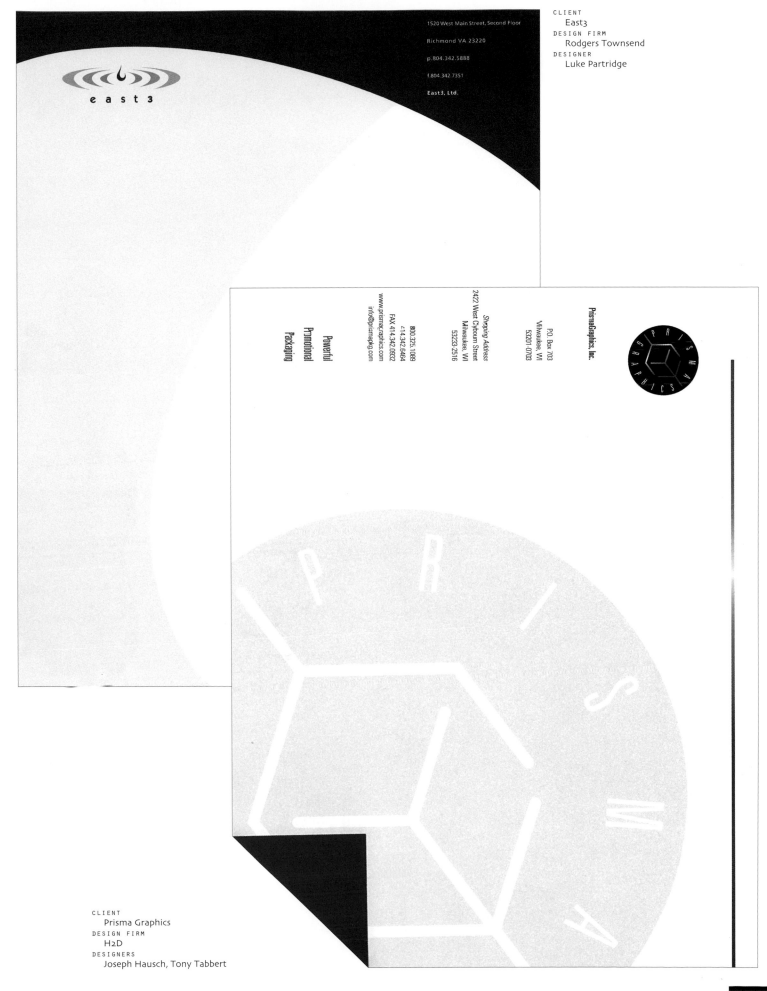

1520 West Main Street, Second Floor

Richmond VA 23220

p.804.342.5888

f.804.342.7351

East3, Ltd.

CLIENT
East3
DESIGN FIRM
Rodgers Townsend
DESIGNER
Luke Partridge

PrismaGraphics, Inc.

P.O. Box 703
Milwaukee, WI
53201-0703

Shipping Address
2422 West Clybourn Street
Milwaukee, WI
53233-2516

800.375.1089
414.342.6464
FAX 414.342.0932
www.prismagraphics.com
info@prismapkg.com

Powerful
Promotional
Packaging

CLIENT
Prisma Graphics
DESIGN FIRM
H2D
DESIGNERS
Joseph Hausch, Tony Tabbert

CLIENT
Marty Doyle Photography
DESIGN FIRM
Adkins/Balchunas
DESIGNERS
Michelle Phaneuf, Jerry Balchunas

MARTY**DOYLE**
*photography*

230 Main Street • Pawtucket, Rhode Island 02860 • TEL/FAX 401.726.7301 • PAGER 401.459.0729

info@webprint.com • www.webprint.com
1142 Cherry Avenue • San Bruno, CA 94066
PHONE: 650-589-0988 • FAX: 650-589-0853

CLIENT
Webprint
DESIGN FIRM
Klundt Hosmer Design
DESIGNERS
Brian Gage, Darin Klundt

CLIENT
 Finian's
DESIGN FIRM
 Adkins/Balchunas
DESIGNERS
 Susan DeAngelis, Jerry Balchunas,
 Michelle Phaneuf

1657 HANCOCK STREET
QUINCY, MA 02169
617-770-2592
Fax 617-770-1260

910 WASHINGTON STREET
DEDHAM, MA 02026
781-329-0097
Fax 781-329-3138

[date ►

[to ►

E

[i]e design

TEL 818 907 8000
FAX 818 907 8830
EMAIL mail@iedesign.net

IE DESIGN 13039 VENTURA BOULEVARD STUDIO CITY, CA 91604

►

E

[i]e design

13039 VENTURA BLVD
STUDIO CITY, CA 91604

CLIENT
 [i]e design
DESIGN FIRM
 [i]e design
DESIGNER
 Marcie Carson

4777 Mallard Cmn. Fremont CA 94555 U.S.A  phone: 510 304 3924 fax: 510 713 2033 www.partyanywhere.com

CLIENT
  Party Anywhere.com
DESIGN FIRM
  Cintara Corporation
DESIGNER
  Nicolette Vandeneynde

party anywhere

PREVAIL

CLIENT
  Party Anywhere.com

THINKING SKILLS THAT FACILITATE INNOVATION.    P. O. Box 100  Marietta, GA 30061-0100

T] 770 426 1008   F] 770 420 8001   www.prevail.org

CLIENT
  Prevail
DESIGN FIRM
  Wages Design
DESIGNER
  Joanna Tak

CLIENT
Aura Estiatorio
DESIGN FIRM
Adkins/Balchunas
DESIGNERS
Susan DeAngelis, Jerry Balchunas

141 EAST 48TH STREET, NEW YORK, NY 10017 TEL 212-759-8550 FAX 212-751-0894

**AccessEdge**

James R. Birch
*President & CEO*

| Mail | 201 Washington Road |
| | Princeton, NJ 08543 |
| Phone | 1.609.734.2193 |
| Fax | 1.609.734.2035 |
| E-mail | jbirch@sarnoff.com |

CLIENT
AccessEdge
DESIGN FIRM
Alan Brooks Design
DESIGNER
Michael Licata

B
A
N
F
F

SPRINGS

**ADVISORY
BOARD**

MARCH 1–4, 2001 • BANFF SPRINGS, CANADA

CLIENT
  Boehringer Ingelheim
  Pharmaceuticals, Inc.
DESIGN FIRM
  Health Science
  Communications, Inc.
DESIGNER
  Robert Padovano

 ScheduleOnline

9606 Aero Drive, Suite 1700   San Diego, CA 92123.1806   Tel: 858.836.4455   Fax: 858.836.4456   www.scheduleonline.com

CLIENT
  ScheduleOnline
DESIGN FIRM
  Bruce Yelaska Design
DESIGNER
  Bruce Yelaska

CLIENT
  coquico
DESIGN FIRM
  Supon Design Group
DESIGNERS
  Supon Phornirunlit,
  Pum Mek-Aroonreung, Lillie Fujinaga

175 STRAFFORD AVENUE
SUITE ONE, PMB 310
WAYNE, PA 19087-3396
TELEPHONE 610 642 9382
FACSIMILE 610 642 8424
www.coquico.com

Barbara Flowers + Associates

*Integrated*
*Design*
*Services*

9050C Cherry Creek Drive South
Denver, Colorado 80231
T 303.751.8697  F 303.368.4161

CLIENT
  Barbara Flowers
DESIGN FIRM
  Noble Erickson, Inc.
DESIGNERS
  Jackie Noble, Robin Ridley

Quality Vision Services, Inc.      716-555-1212
1175 North Street                  Fax: 716-555-1313
Rochester, New York 14621 USA      www.qvsmeasurement.com

Quality
Vision
Services

BILL GOULD DESIGN
ART & ARCHITECTURE

14107-P WINCHESTER BLVD
LOS GATOS, CA 95030
FAX 408.871.3149
PHONE 408.871.3140

Quality Vision International

Quality Vision Services, Inc.

Optical Gaging Products

VIEW Engineering

**Davies Associates**

Environmental & Corporate Graphics

9424 Dayton Way
Suite 217
Beverly Hills, CA 90210

tel 310.247.9572
fax 310.247.9590

www.daviesla.com

CLIENT
Davies Associates
DESIGN FIRM
Davies Associates
DESIGNERS
J. Andrew Podrutt, Cathy Davies

gina vance

gina vance

800 Wellsford Road
Modesto, CA 95357
209.527.9761

CLIENT
Gina Vance
DESIGN FIRM
Never Boring Design
DESIGNER
Jason Pillon

**Dental Concepts**  650 From Road  Ph 201 576 9700
Paramus  Fx 201 576 9780
New Jersey  em dentalconcepts@dentalconcepts.com
07652

CLIENT
Dental Concepts, Inc.
DESIGN FIRM
Handler Design Group, Inc.
DESIGNER
Bruce Handler

MARKETBRIDGE

4550 MONTGOMERY AVENUE, 500 NORTH TOWER  |  BETHESDA, MARYLAND 20814
P: 301.907.3800  |  F: 301.907.3282  |  W: www.market-bridge.com

CLIENT
Market Bridge
DESIGN FIRM
West + Associates
DESIGNER
Carolanne O'Neil

CLIENT
Cipriani Kremer Design
DESIGN FIRM
Cipriani Kremer Design
DESIGNERS
Tom Bowerman, John Weber

**c kd**

Cipriani Kremer Design

www.ckdesign.com

P **617 587 8800**
F 617 587 8855

Twc Copley Place Boston Massachusetts **02116**

A division of Arnold Communications, Inc.

# JIM PRATER
## BUILDER/CARPENTER, INC.

1421 TRENTON-HARBOURTON ROAD • PENNINGTON, NEW JERSEY 08534 • 609-737-7386 • FAX: 609-737-8512

CLIENT
Jim Prater
DESIGN FIRM
Zoe Graphics
DESIGNERS
Kim Waters, Kathy Pagano

CLIENT
Vigilo
DESIGN FIRM
H2D
DESIGNERS
Joseph Hausch, Jennifer Peck

Vigilo, Inc.

10558 N. Port Washington Rd.

Mequon, WI 53092-5537

**262-240-0760**

Fax: 262-240-0761

www.vigilonet.com

Methodologie, Inc. 808 Howell St., Ste. 600 Seattle, WA 98101 www.methodologie.com 206.623.1044 206.625.0154 fax

Methodologie

creative catalyst

Methodologie, Inc. 808 Howell St., Ste. 600 Seattle, WA 98101

CLIENT
Methodologie, Inc.
DESIGN FIRM
Methodologie, Inc.
DESIGNER
Daniele Monti

CLIENT
  Aubase Aviation
DESIGN FIRM
  Design Room
DESIGNER
  Chad Gordon

AVBASE
A V I A T I O N

I-X JET CENTER
6200 RIVERSIDE DRIVE
CLEVELAND, OHIO 44135

T] 216-265-9500
T] 800-294-5387
F] 216-265-9501
W] WWW.AVBASE.COM

415 957-1975
415 957-1976

www.scienceandfiction.com

164 townsend street #4 san francisco CA 94107

SCIENCE AND FICTION
a rare medium company

164 townsend street #4 san francisco CA 94107

SCIENCE AND FICTION
a rare medium company

www.scienceandfiction.com

* elliptical correction of eluding posse-i.e. 'doubling back'

CLIENT
  Rare Science & Fiction
DESIGN FIRM
  Cahan and Associates
DESIGNERS
  Jean Orlebeke, Bill Cahan

# Telaric

INNOVATION TO VENTURE CAPITAL

**Telaric, LLC**
10558 N Port Washington Road
Mequon, WI 53092

P: 262-240-0760
F: 262-240-0761

www.telaric.com

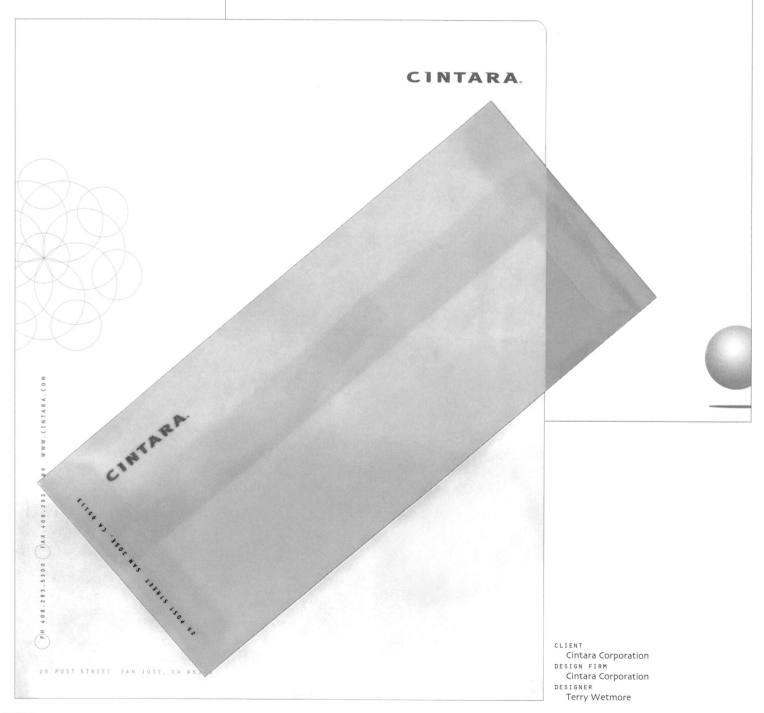

# CINTARA.

CINTARA.

PH 408.293.5300 FAX 408.293.89 WWW.CINTARA.COM

25 POST STREET SAN JOSE, CA 95113

FOOD LABEL & PACKAGE DESIGN

CLIENT
Seven Course Design
DESIGN FIRM
Graif Design
DESIGNER
Matt Graif

**MICHAEL TOMPERT**
DIGITAL IMAGE & VIDEO ARTIST

PICTURES OF THE MIND'S EYE

216 FULTON STREET | PALO ALTO, CALIFORNIA 94301 | PHONE 650.323.0365 | FAX 650.323.0366 | EMAIL MICHAEL@TOMPERT.COM

**MICHAEL TOMPERT**
DIGITAL IMAGE & VIDEO ARTIST

216 FULTON | PALO ALTO | CA 94301
PHONE 650.323.0365
EMAIL MICHAEL@TOMPERT.COM
WEBSITE WWW.TOMPERT.COM

MICHAEL TOMPERT
216 FULTON STREET | CALIFORNIA 94301
PALO ALTO

CLIENT
Michael Tompert
DESIGN FIRM
Tompertdesign
DESIGNERS
Claudia Huber Tompert,
Michael Tompert

VIVE LA FRANCE

CLIENT
Paris Casino Resort
DESIGN FIRM
David Carter Design Associates
DESIGNER
Ashley B. Mattocks

*vive las vegas*
LA JOIE DE VIVRE

VENDARIA

PARIS LAS VEGAS
3655 Las Vegas Boulevard, South
Las Vegas, Nevada 89109
Telephone 702.946.7000
Facsimile 702.946.4405

CLIENT
Vendaria
DESIGN FIRM
Methodologie, Inc.
DESIGNERS
Gabe Goldman, Hugh Rodman

316 Occidental Ave. S 2nd Floor Seattle Washington 98104 [tel: 206 223.4000 fax: 206 381.0806 net: www.vendaria.com]

CLIENT
Hotspring
DESIGN FIRM
BTD
DESIGNERS
BTD nyc, Beth Tondreau,
Daniel Rodney

CLIENT
Children's Museum (CM2)
DESIGN FIRM
Grady Britton
DESIGNER
Jeni Stewart

3037 SW SECOND AVENUE    PORTLAND, OREGON 97201    503.823.2227 P    503.823.3667 F

CLIENT
Virtuoso
DESIGN FIRM
David Carter Design Associates
DESIGNER
Ashley B. Mattocks

# VIRTUOSO
SPECIALISTS IN THE ART OF TRAVEL

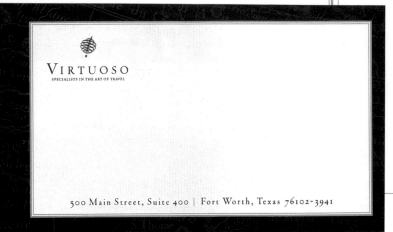

# VIRTUOSO
SPECIALISTS IN THE ART OF TRAVEL

500 Main Street, Suite 400 | Fort Worth, Texas 76102-3941

U.S. ADVISOR

500 Main Street, Suite 400 | Fort Worth, Texas 76102-3941
information@virtuoso.com   www.virtuoso.com
817-870-0300 Telephone   817-870-1050 Facsimile

CLIENT
U.S. Advisor
DESIGN FIRM
Mastandrea Design, Inc.
DESIGNER
Mary Anne Mastandrea

**U.S. Advisor LLC**
3108-B Fillmore Street, San Francisco, CA 94123
TEL 415 202-8941 FAX 415 202-8942 www.usreit.com

CLIENT
Abacus
DESIGN FIRM
David Carter Design Associates
DESIGNER
Emily Cain

ABACUS

4511 McKinney Avenue Dallas, Texas 75205 P. 214.559.3111 F.214.559.3113

4511 McKinney Avenue Dallas, Texas 75205

ABACUS

abacus-restaurant.com

kirlin
foundation

CLIENT
The Kirlin Foundation
DESIGN FIRM
Methodologie, Inc.
DESIGNERS
Gabe Goldman, Christopher Downs

Kirlin Foundation 10230 NE Points Dr. Suite 500 Kirkland WA 98033 tel/fax 206 381 2251 web www.kirlinfoundation.org

CLASSIC CREST

CLIENT
Moca Online
DESIGN FIRM
Supon Design Group
DESIGNERS
Supon Phornirunlit, Lillie Fuginaga

M O
C A
ONLINE.COM

**MUSEUM OF COLLECTIBLE ARTS ONLINE**
1523 P ST, NW, WASHINGTON, DC 20005
TEL: 202.667.1752  FAX: 202.234.1466
E-MAIL: MOCASHOP@AOL.COM
WWW.MOCAONLINE.COM

CLIENT
Chimayo At the Beach
DESIGN FIRM
On The Edge Design
DESIGNERS
Tracey Lamberson, Jeff Gasper

315 Pacific Coast Hwy. ★ Huntington Beach, CA 92648 ★ Ph: 714.374.7273 Fax: 714.374.7263

11 Sixth Road
Woburn, MA 01801
Tel 781.932.8882
Fax 781.932.8889
**www.planetpackaging.com**

CLIENT
Planet Packaging.com
DESIGN FIRM
Gold Forest Advertising
DESIGNERS
Ray Garcia, Tony Persiani,
Michael Gold, Lauren Gold

*Where Art Meets It's Maker*

Ryon Rich

RR 31 Box 330C
Santa Fe, NM
87505
505.471.5678
www.rynofab.com

Fine Art Bronze and Metal Fabrication

RYNO**FAB**

CLIENT
Rynofab
DESIGN FIRM
Stephanie Cunningham
DESIGNER
Stephanie Cunningham

**IntegraTech**

2677 Roundhill Circle
Placerville, CA 95667-8737

www.integratech.net

*tele/fax:* 530.622.5424

CLIENT
IntegraTech
DESIGN FIRM
Gage Design
DESIGNER
Chris Roberts

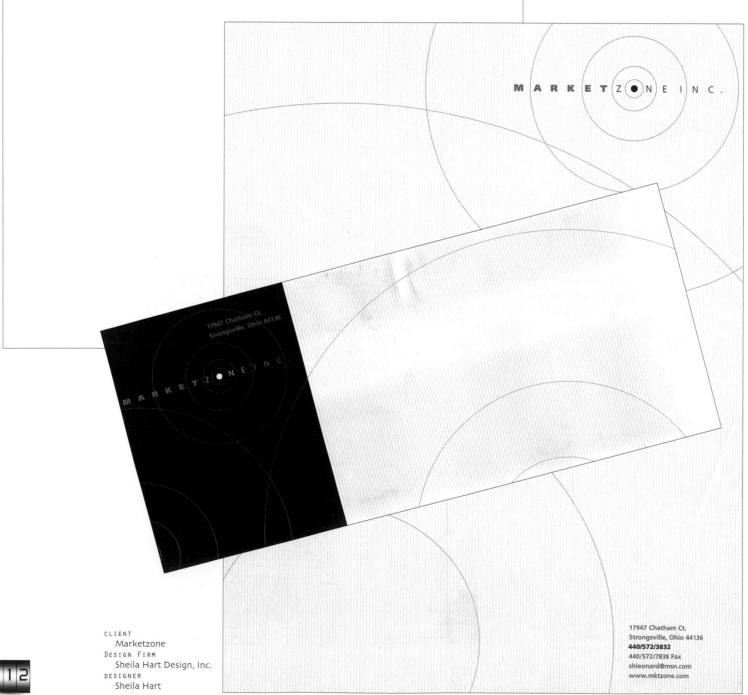

CLIENT
Marketzone
DESIGN FIRM
Sheila Hart Design, Inc.
DESIGNER
Sheila Hart

CLIENT
Innovative Media Research
DESIGN FIRM
Peterson & Co.
DESIGNER
Bryan Peterson

Innovative Media Research

2427 Allen Street, Suite 229
Dallas, Texas 75204
Phone: 214 908-6942
E-mail: tmcgee@imrc.com

Disneyland® Resort Marketing

The Beach

P. O. Box 3232

Anaheim, California

92803-3232

Press & Publicity - Disneyland. Resort - P.O. Box 3232, Anaheim, California 92803-3232 - (714) 781-4500

©Disney

CLIENT
Disneyland Resort Marketing
JJ Buettgen/Liz Gill
DESIGN FIRM
Disneyland Resort
Creative Print Services
DESIGNERS
Dathan Shore, Scott Starkey

*Avicon*

CLIENT
Avicon
DESIGN FIRM
Doerr Associates
DESIGNER
Lauren Jevick

www.avicon.com

Suite 200
555 Republic Drive
Plano, TX
75074
972.516.4232

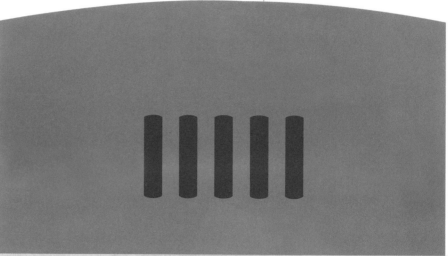

impli

Nate Goore
534 Fourth Street
San Francisco, CA 94107
t: 415.972.1050
f: 415.972.1099
e: ngoore@impli.com
w: www.impli.com

Connecting eye to i

CLIENT
Impli
DESIGN FIRM
Hornall Anderson
Design Works, Inc.
DESIGNERS
Jack Anderson, Debra McCloskey,
Anne Johnston, Tobi Brown,
Henry Yiu, John Anderle

# CHICAGO
CONVENTION AND TOURISM BUREAU

CLIENT
Chicago Convention & Tourism
Bureau
DESIGN FIRM
Davis Harrison Dion
DESIGNERS
Bob Dion, Dave Paoletti

2301 South Lake Shore Drive

Chicago, IL 60616-1490

Phone: 312-567-8500

Fax: 312-567-8533

choosechicago.com

SUPON PHORNIRUNLIT • 1523 P STREET, NW • WASHINGTON, DC 20005 • TEL: 202.667.1752 • E-MAIL: KHUNSUPON@AOL.COM • WWW.SUPON.COM/COLLECTINGEVERYTHING

SUPON PHORNIRUNLIT • 1523 P STREET, NW • WASHINGTON, DC 20005

SUPON PHORNIRUNLIT

COLLECTING EVERYTHING

COLLECTING
EVERYTHING
SUPON PHORNIRUNLIT
1523 P ST. NW
WASHINGTON, DC 20005
TEL: 202.667.1752
E-MAIL: KHUNSUPON@AOL.COM
WWW.SUPON.COM/COLLECTINGEVERYTHING

COLLECTING EVERYTHING

CLIENT
Collecting Everything
DESIGN FIRM
Supon Design Group
DESIGNER
Supon Phornirulit,
Pum Mek-Aroonreung

FUZE TECHNOLOGIES | 217 Pine Street, Suite 600 Seattle, WA 98101 | P 206.447.1889  F 206.447.9571 | www.fuze.com

fuze

FUZE TECHNOLOGIES | 217 Pine Street, Suite 600 Seattle, WA 98101 | www.fuze.com

fuze

Centegy
Integrated e-Business Solutions

6539A Dumbarton Circle  Fremont, CA 94555 USA  Phone: 510.789.1820  Fax: 510.789.1850  www.centegy.com

CLIENT
Tosca Radigonda Photography
DESIGN FIRM
Interbrand Hulefeld
DESIGNER
Anita Betz

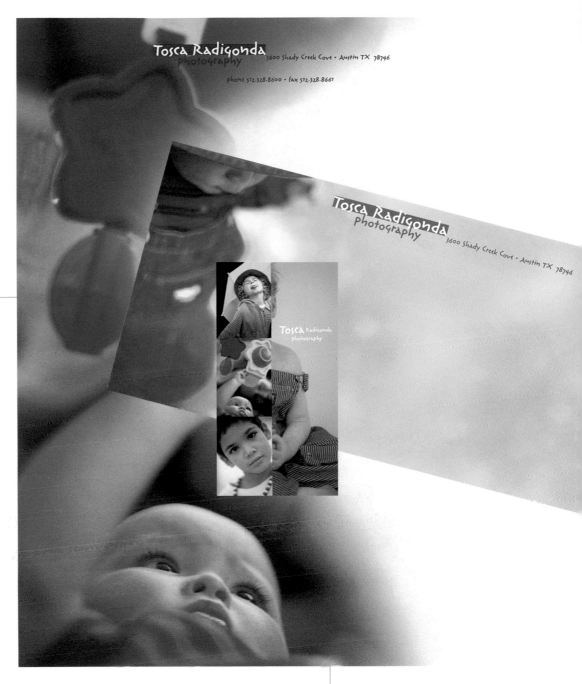

CLIENT
LSY interactive
DESIGN FIRM
Lord, Sullivan & Yoder
Marketing Communications
DESIGNERS
Michael Wheatley, Hugh Collins

CLIENT
Tango Cat
DESIGN FIRM
Paradowski Graphic Design
DESIGNER
Shawn Cornell

T a n g o • c a t ℠

The Nexus of Enterprise and the Arts

tangocat.com

fax 314 963 7747

314 963 7763

315 Marion Avenue   Saint Louis, MO 63119-2616

Sf
Sample First™
corporation

P.O. Box 724 • Lewiston, NY 14092-0724
ph:716.754.7640 • fx:716.754.2700
email:sample1st@worldnet.att.net
web:www.sample1st.com

Sample Partners Worldwide™

CLIENT
Sample First Corporation
DESIGN FIRM
McElveney & Palozzi
Design Group, Inc.
DESIGNERS
Kristen Quackenbush,
Lisa Williamson

CLIENT
Bulabay
DESIGN FIRM
1185 Design
DESIGNERS
Peggy Burke, Julia Foug,
Merry Biggerstaff

**BULABAY**™

WILLIAM G. BARTON
**Chairman of the Board &
Chief Executive Officer**

**[86].COM**

1341 G STREET, NW
SUITE 1100
WASHINGTON, DC 20005

**PHONE:** 202.585.0286
**FAX:** 202.393.0712
**E-MAIL:** INFO@86.COM

**a** 2999 Oak Road
Suite 300
Walnut Creek, CA
94596

bbarton@bulabay.com **e**

**p** 925.287.8717 x106

**f** 925.287.8708

CLIENT
86.com
DESIGN FIRM
Gibson Creative
DESIGNER
Juliette Brown

CLIENT
Arbor South
DESIGN FIRM
Funk and Associates
DESIGNER
Chris Berner

4765 VILLAGE PLAZA LOOP
SUITE 200
Eugene, Oregon 97401

541-344-3332

CLIENT
French 75 Restaurant
DESIGN FIRM
On The Edge Design
DESIGNERS
Jeff Gasper, Gina Mims

1464 S. Pacific Coast Hwy

Laguna Beach, CA 92651

Phone: 714-494-8444

Fax: 714-494-7004

CLIENT
Black Bear Gallery
DESIGN FIRM
Lomangino Studio Inc.
DESIGNER
Kim Pollock

360 MAIN STREET  P.O. BOX 478  WASHINGTON, VA 22747
T 540 675 3636  F 540 675 2346

BARNES NURSERY INC,    3511 West Cleveland Rd. Huron, Ohio 44839
419 433 5525 *phone*  800 421 8722 *toll free*  419 433 3555 *fax*

L A N D S C A P I N G   M A I N T E N A N C E   L A W N   C A R E   T R E E   C A R E   P R O D U C T I O N   N U R S E R Y   O R G A N I C S   R E C O V E R Y

CLIENT
Barnes Nursery Inc.
DESIGN FIRM
Epstein Design Partners
DESIGNER
Gina Linchon

CATAWBA GARDEN CENTER
1283 N.E. Catawba Rd., SR 53 Port Clinton, Ohio 43452
419 797 9797 *phone*  419 797 9716 *fax*

**BAUGH**

**CONSTRUCTION**

CLIENT
Baugh
DESIGN FIRM
NBBJ Graphic Design
DESIGNER
Roddy Grant

**900 Poplar Place South** Seattle
206.726.8000 206.328.9235 fax
www.baughent.com

151 FIRST AVENUE, PH-1
NEW YORK, NY 10003
PHONE: 212-979-2661 FAX: 212-260-3525
WWW.KELLUMMCCLAIN.COM

Kellum McClain Inc.

MAIL: P.O. BOX 148
COURIER: 1541 COUNTY RTE. 5 SO.
CANAAN, NY 12029
PHONE+FAX: 518-781-3439

Kellum

151 FIRST AVENUE, PH-1
NEW YORK, NY 10003
PHONE: 212-979-2661
FAX: 212-260-3525
EMAIL: RON@KELLUMMCCLAIN.COM

**Ron Kellum**

MAIL: P.O. BOX 148
COURIER: 1541 COUNTY RTE. 5 SO.
CANAAN, NY 12029
PHONE+FAX: 518-781-3439

CLIENT
Kellum McClain, Inc.
DESIGN FIRM
Kellum McClain, Inc.
DESIGNER
Ron Kellum

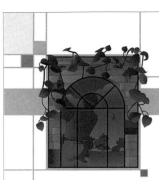

EXPERTS' ROUNDTABLE
New Developments in LMWH Use for Orthopedics
*Four Seasons Las Colinas • February 2-4, 2001*

CLIENT
Pharmacia Corporation
DESIGN FIRM
Health Science Communications, Inc.
DESIGNER
Robert Padovano

visual asylum 205 WEST DATE SAN DIEGO CA 92101

visual asylum 205 WEST DATE SAN DIEGO CA 92101 T 619.233.9633 F 619.233.9637

CLIENT
Visual Asylum
DESIGN FIRM
Visual Asylum
DESIGNERS
Joel Sotelo, MaeLin Levine

kedestra

CLIENT
Kedestra
DESIGN FIRM
BBK Studio
DESIGNERS
Yang Kim, Kelly Schwartz

13400 Bishop's Lane
Brookfield WI 53005
(262) 814-1800
fax (262) 814-9936

BRAIN**RANGER**

6080 Greenwood Plaza Blvd · Englewood, CO 80111 · 303.268.4470 · Fax 303.268.4415 · www.brainranger.com

CLIENT
Brain Ranger
DESIGN FIRM
Rassman Design
DESIGNERS
John Rassman, Glen Hobbs

CLIENT
Kedestra
DESIGN FIRM
BBK Studio

espriTV

CLIENT
ESPritv
DESIGN FIRM
Sargent & Berman
DESIGNER
Jelina Saurenmann

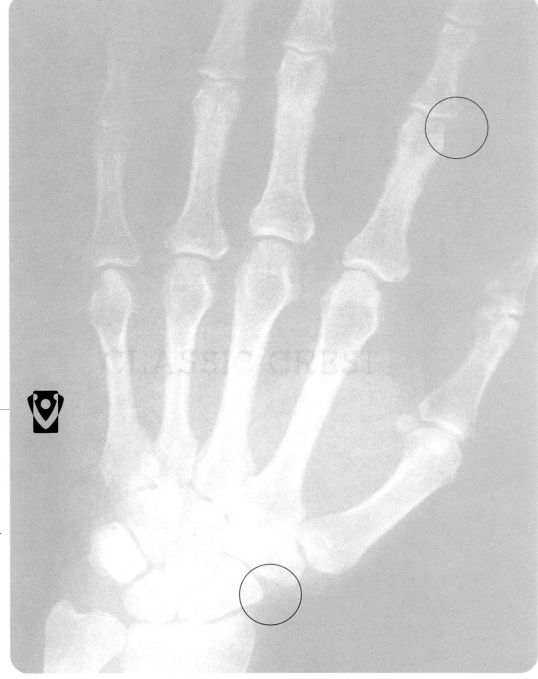

EspriTV, Inc.
1875 Century Park East, Suite 1320
Los Angeles, California 90067
T | 310.277.3888   F | 310.277.8282
E | info@espritv.com

CLIENT
CVIA Central Vally Imaging Assoc.
DESIGN FIRM
Never Boring Design Associates
DESIGNER
Jason Pillen

509•324•9256 / fax 509•323•8979 / www.leehayes.com

lee & hayes pllc, intellectual property law

421 west riverside avenue, suite 500, spokane, washington 99201

lee&hayes

CLIENT
Lee & Hayes, PLLC
DESIGN FIRM
Klundt Hosmer Design
DESIGNER
Darin Klundt

PRISM
WORLDWIDE, INC

MIAMI

TAIPEI

HONG KONG

QINGDAO

CLIENT
Prism Worldwide, Inc.
DESIGN FIRM
Gouthier Design, Inc.
DESIGNER
Jonathan J. Gouthier

2875 NORTH EAST 191ST STREET, SUITE 402    AVENTURA, FLORIDA 33180    PH 305 933-0222    FX 305 956-2386

CLIENT
  RMB Vivid
DESIGN FIRM
  RMB Vivid
DESIGNERS
  Brian Boram, Robert Meador,
  Keith Rea

1932 First Avenue

Number 607

Seattle, Washington

USA 98101

206 956 0688 Voice

206 956 0619 Fax

www.rmbvivid.com

RMB**Vivid**

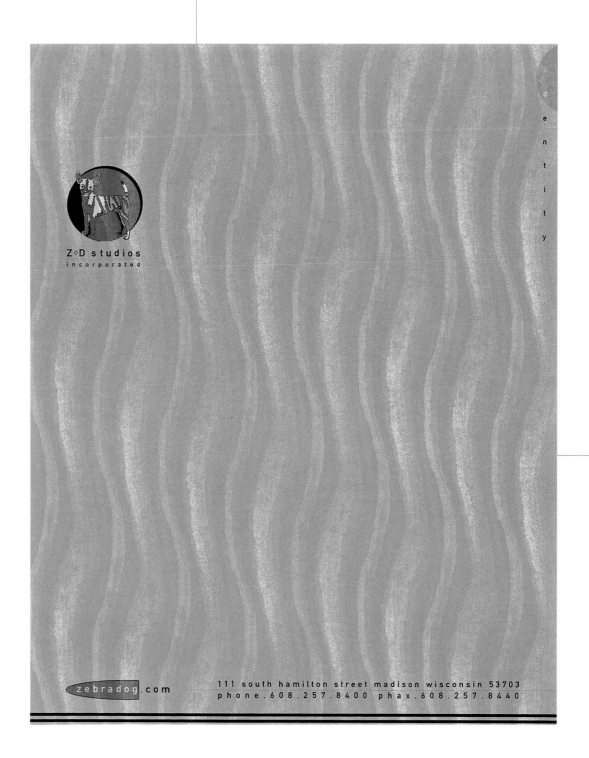

Z○D studios
incorporated

identity

REA, MEADOR, BORAM

zebradog.com

111 south hamilton street madison wisconsin 53703
phone.608.257.8400 phax.608.257.8440

CLIENT
  Z•D Studios
DESIGN FIRM
  Z•D Studios
DESIGNER
  Mark Schmitz

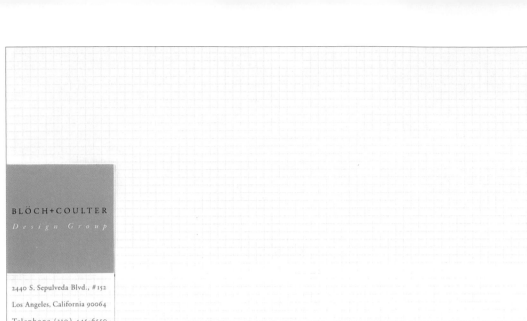

BLÖCH+COULTER
*Design Group*

2440 S. Sepulveda Blvd., #152
Los Angeles, California 90064
Telephone (310) 445-6550
Facsimile (310) 445-6555
admin@blochcoulter.com
www.blochcoulter.com

CLIENT
Blöch + Coulter Design Group
DESIGN FIRM
Blöch + Coulter Design Group
DESIGNER
Thomas Blöch, Ellie Young Suh

**Susan Northrop Design**
*Graphic Communications*

Carriage Dr.
Lincoln, RI 02865
Tel. 401.727.9227
Fax. 401.727.9203

CLIENT
Susan Northrop Design
DESIGN FIRM
Susan Northrop Design
DESIGNER
Susan Northrop

CLIENT
Viadesign
DESIGN FIRM
Viadesign
DESIGNERS
Marc Hawkins,
Theresa Vandenberg

THE ART OF VISION

The Wahl Group

WILD APPLE

WILD APPLE
526 Woodstock Road
Woodstock, Vermont 05091

tel 802-457-3003
800-756-8359
fax 802-457/ 3214
800-411-2775
email Sales@WildApple.com

www.WildApple.com

art of vision

10453 La Morada Drive / San Diego, CA 92124 / 858-715-1957 / www.theartofvision.com

526 WOODSTOCK ROAD · WOODSTOCK, VERMONT 05091
TEL 802-457-3003    FAX 802-457-3214
WWW.WILDAPPLE.COM

CLIENT
Wild Apple Graphics
DESIGN FIRM
Wild Apple Graphics
DESIGNER
Sue Schlabach

**SCHWENKE**
DESIGN & BUILD, INC

607 KATHRYN
NIXA, MO 65714
417.725.6726
FAX.724.2811

CLIENT
Schwendi Design & Build
DESIGN FIRM
Graif Design
DESIGNER
Matt Graif

TTA
THE TATE AGENCY
INTEGRATED ADVERTISING AND MARKETING

1000 ST. ALBANS DRIVE • SUITE 350 • RALEIGH, NC • 27609

CLIENT
The Tate Agency
DESIGN FIRM
The Tate Agency
DESIGNER
Julie A. Schaffroth

1000 ST. ALBANS DRIVE • SUITE 350 • RALEIGH, NC • 27609 • p 919 878 0020 • f 919 878 0327 • www.thetateagency.com

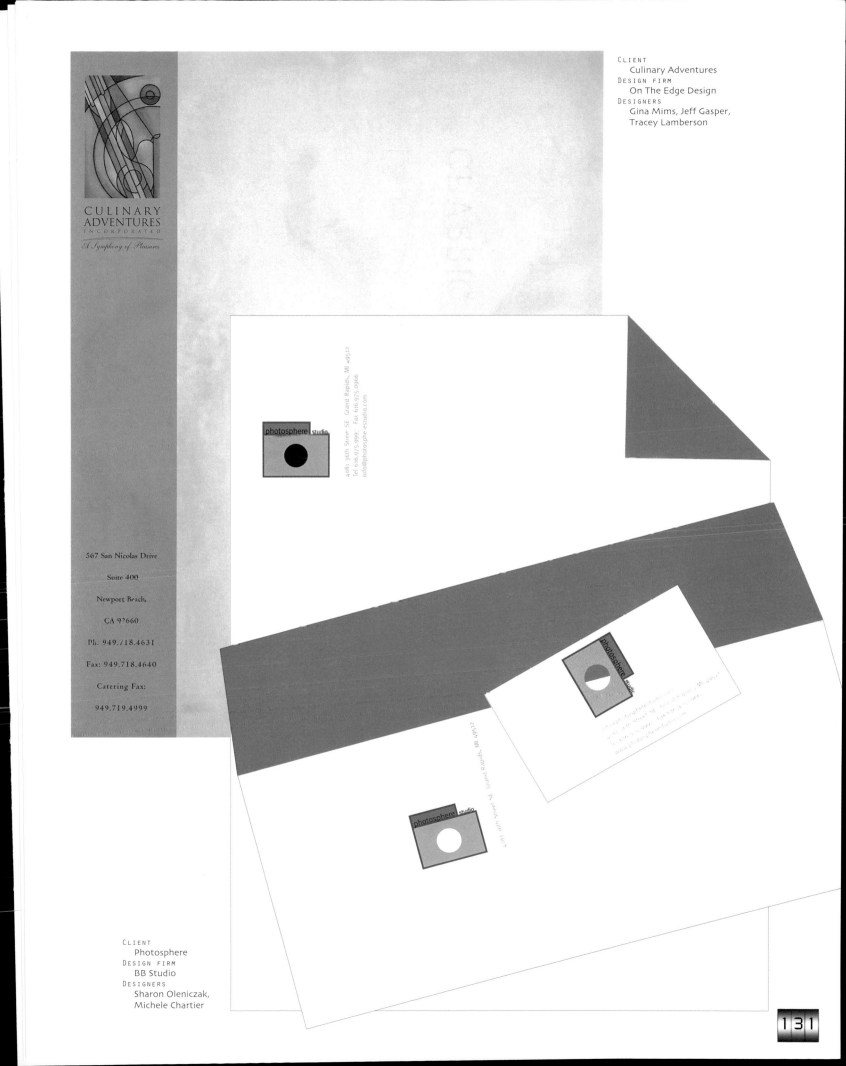

CULINARY
ADVENTURES
INCORPORATED

*A Symphony of Pleasures*

567 San Nicolas Drive

Suite 400

Newport Beach,

CA 92660

Ph. 949.718.4631

Fax: 949.718.4640

Catering Fax:

949.719.4999

CLIENT
  Culinary Adventures
DESIGN FIRM
  On The Edge Design
DESIGNERS
  Gina Mims, Jeff Gasper,
  Tracey Lamberson

photosphere studio

4081 36th Stree SE  Grand Rapids,, MI 49512
Tel 616.975.999.  Fax 616.975.0966
info@photosphe estudio.com

CLIENT
  Photosphere
DESIGN FIRM
  BB Studio
DESIGNERS
  Sharon Oleniczak,
  Michele Chartier

131

CLIENT
  3osixty design, inc.
DESIGN FIRM
  3osixty design, inc.
DESIGNERS
  Pär larsson, Henry Vizcarm

**Nkey**

productions
music
studios

p.o. box 843
troy, ohio 45373
p&f 937•339•3903

www.30sixtydesign.com   2801 cahuenga blvd. west   los angeles, ca 90068   voice 323 850 5311   fax 323 850 6638

CLIENT
  Nkey Productions,
  Music & Studios
DESIGN FIRM
  Anise V. Simpson
  Graphic Designer/Illustrator
DESIGNER
  Anise V. Simpson

CLIENT
  Dietz Design
DESIGN FIRM
  Dietz Design
DESIGNERS
  Robert Dietz, Kathy Thompson,
  Dannielle Moilanen

DIETZ DESIGN COMPANY

DIETZ DESIGN COMPANY

80 SOUTH JACKSON SUITE 308 SEATTLE WA 98104   T 206.621.1855  F 206.621.7146   WWW.DIETZDESIGN.COM

portable life

*Mobility starts here*

www.portablelife.com

20100 Stevens Creek Blvd., Suite 200      Ph: 408.861.1500
Cupertino, CA  95014                      Fx: 408.861.1501

CLIENT
  Portable Life.com
DESIGN FIRM
  Howry Design Associates
DESIGNERS
  Jill Howry, Clay Williams

CLIENT
    Madison Symphony Orchestra
DESIGN FIRM
    Z•D Studios
DESIGNER
    Mark Schmitz

John DeMain ı Music Director

211 North Carroll Street ı Madison, Wisconsin 53703 ı 608.257.3734 ı fax 608.258.2315 ı www.madisonsymphony.org

CLIENT
    Cobion
DESIGN FIRM
    Visigy
DESIGNER
    Chelsea Hernandez

POST 703 Market St. Ste. 1011 San Francisco, CA 94103 USA ı FON 415.272.2088 ı FAX 415.979.9322 ı URL www.cobion.com

CLIENT
**Street Mail**
DESIGN FIRM
Corey McPherson Nash
DESIGNER
Dan Kennedy

60 E 42nd Street
Eighth Floor
New York, NY 10165
☎ 212-981-2570
🖷 212-981-1986

www.streetmail.com

CLIENT
**RxKinetix, Inc.**
DESIGN FIRM
Asher Studio
DESIGNERS
Russ Chilcoat, Connie Asher

RxKinetix, Inc.          1172 Century Drive · Suite 260 · Louisville, Colorado 80027 U.S.A.
                         T 303.926.1900 · F 303.926.1906 · www.rxkinetix.com

CLIENT
Smarteam Communications Inc.
DESIGN FIRM
Smarteam Communications Inc.
DESIGNERS
Gary Ridley, Marcos Ballestero

>LOST
>FOUND...
>RETURNED!

CLIENT
Stuffbak.com
DESIGN FIRM
CommArts, Inc.
DESIGNERS
Henry Beer, Eric Fowles

7960 NIWOT RD. BLDG. B12, NIWOT, CO 80503 | PH:303.652.0800 | FAX:303.652.0855 | WWW.STUFFBAK.COM

CLIENT
Veracity Capital Partners
DESIGN FIRM
Baker Designed Communications
DESIGNER
Brian Keenan

VERACITY
CAPITAL PARTNERS

Ruetschle Architects

www.vc.com

VERACITY
CAPITAL PARTNERS

283 Dartmouth Street
Boston, MA 02116

VERACITY
CAPITAL PARTNERS

One Market Plaza
Steuart Street Tower
Suite 1225
San Francisco, CA 94105
TEL (415) 247-1077
FAX (415) 247-1096

283 Dartmouth Street
Boston, MA 02116
WEB www.vc.com
TEL (617) 424-9135
FAX (617) 424-9158

CLIENT
Ruetschle Architects
DESIGN FIRM
Visual Marketing Associates, Inc.
DESIGNERS
Amy Baas, Steve Goubeaux

222 Linwood Street  Dayton, Ohio  45405-4943
t: 937.461.5390  f: 937.461.6829  w: www.ruetschle.com

CLIENT
Rainbow Signs, Inc.
DESIGN FIRM
Rainbow Signs, Inc.
DESIGNERS
Lynda Riley, Margo DePaulis,
Terri Wille

3500 Thurston Avenue

Anoka . Minnesota

5 5 3 0 3 ~ 1 0 6 1

Ph 612.576.6700

Fx 612.576.6701

1.800.544.6846

Screen Print

Creative

Custom Signs

Digital

acoustiguide

**Acoustiguide Corporation**
330 Seventh Avenue, 17th Floor, New York, NY 10001 USA **T** 212.279.1300 **F** 212.279.8520 **E** info@acoustiguide.com
*New York  Washington D.C.  San Francisco  London  Berlin  Amsterdam  Milan  Taipei  Shanghai  Beijing  Tokyo  Sydney*

CLIENT
Acoustiguide Corporation
DESIGN FIRM
Russell Design Associates
DESIGNER
Tina Winey

CLIENT
Culbertson + Jordan
DESIGN FIRM
Never Boring Design Associates
DESIGNER
Melody MacMurry

Culbertson Jordan

Dennis J. Culbertson, C.P.A.
Mark W. Jordan, C.P.A.
Julia G. Jordan, C.P.A.
Marlene R. Culbertson, E.A.

819 17th Street
Modesto, CA 95354

209.544.8150
fax. 209.544.8152

www.culbertsonjordan.com

Certified Public Accountants

Global Bay

111 John Street, Suite 650
New York, NY 10038

℗ 212 · 791 · 1369
℗ 212 · 202 · 4966

www.globalbay.com

CLIENT
Global Bay
DESIGN FIRM
LiquidZReality
DESIGNERS
Carlos Gonzalez, Jason Guzman

Suka & Friends Design, Inc.
560 Broadway
Suite 307
New York, NY 10012

212.219.0082
212.219.0699
friends@sukadesign.com

CLIENT
Suka & Friends Design, Inc.
DESIGN FIRM
Suka & Friends Design, Inc.
DESIGNER
Sean Garretson

AKRON AIRSHIP HISTORICAL CENTER

CLIENT
Akron Airship Historical Center
DESIGN FIRM
Wilhelm Design
DESIGNER
Jeff Wilhelm

P. O. Box 9127 Akron, Ohio 44305

CLIENT
The LTC Group
DESIGN FIRM
The LTC Group/Liquid Graphix

**THE LTC GROUP**

+ □ ılı ○

*dever designs*

**headquarters**

| | |
|---|---|
| main | 972.714.4800 |
| toll free | 800.365.8957 |
| fax | 972.714.4000 |
| web | www.ltcgroup.com |
| 2010 westridge drive | irving, tx 75038 |

CLIENT
The LTC Group
DESIGN FIRM
The LTC Group/Liquid Graphix

1056 WEST STREET, LAUREL, MD 20707 ■ TEL 301-776-2812 ■ FAX 301-953-1196

CLIENT
Dever Designs
DESIGN FIRM
Dever Designs
DESIGNER
Jeffrey L. Dever

"We are what we repeatedly do.
Excellence, then, is not an act, but a habit."
-Aristotle

www.unifiedfield.com

unified_field

T_  212 . 532 . 9595     F_  212 . 532 . 9667     E_  info@unifiedfield.com     3 east 28th street     9th floor     new york, ny   10016

CLIENT
  Unified Field
DESIGN FIRM
  Unified Field
DESIGNER
  Leslie A. Gubitosi

DCA LANDSCAPE ARCHITECTS, INC.

DCA
LANDSCAPE
ARCHITECTS,
INC.

CLIENT
  DCA Landscape Architects
DESIGN FIRM
  Martin-Schaffer, Inc.
DESIGNER
  Adrianne Wright

1315 WISCONSIN AVE. NW, WASHINGTON D.C. 20007
P: 202.337.1160   F: 202.337.4630
gardens@dcalandarch.com   www.dcalandarch.com

CLIENT
  Cool Strategies
DESIGN FIRM
  Strata-Media, Inc.
DESIGNERS
  Dean Del Sesto, Anita Zulkarnain,
  Lauren Ivy

cool strategies

cool strategies™

P.O. Box 1657
Brea, CA 92822-1657
tel: (714) 990-5701
cell phone: (714) 329-9984
www.coolstrategies.com

deedee@coolstrategies.com

**Deedee Snyder, Navigator**
*Network Blue*

P.O. Box 1657
Brea, CA 92822-1657
tel: (714) 990-5701
www.coolstrategies.com

CLIENT
  Eikon Properties
DESIGN FIRM
  FutureBrand HyperMedia
DESIGNERS
  Anna Shteerman, Monse Miguell

88 King Street I SF I CA I 94107 I 415.371.8800 I www.liveatONE.com

ONE
EMBARCADERO SOUTH

CLIENT
  Culinary Revolution
DESIGN FIRM
  Gauger & Silva
DESIGNER
  Isabelle LaPorte

CULINARY REVOLUTION

1320 Inspiration Drive
La Jolla, CA 92037
Telephone: 858•551•7643
Facsimile: 858•454•1688
harrycoplan@chefakasha.com

digital solutions group

THE**LTC**GROUP

main        312.922.8816
toll free   800.497.2695
fax         312.922.6822
web         www.dsgsolutions.com
815 south jefferson street | chicago, il 60607

CLIENT
  The LTC Group
DESIGN FIRM
  The LTC Group/Liquid Grafix

CLIENT
CreAgri
DESIGN FIRM
Mastandrea Design, Inc.
DESIGNER
MaryAnne Mastandrea

digitango

CreAgri, LLC | 25551 Whitesell Street | Hayward, CA 94545
tel 510-732-6478 | fax 510-732-6493 | email creagri.com

THE LTC GROUP

+ ☐ ▥ ○

main 415.970.3344
fax 415.970.2388
web www.digitango.com
1302 22nd street san francisco, ca 94107

CLIENT
The LTC Group
DESIGN FIRM
The LTC Group/Liquid Graphix

ph 540/338.0717
fx 540/338.0737
www.brohard.com

brohard design

CLIENT
  Brohard Designs
DESIGN FIRM
  Broahard Designs Inc.
DESIGNER
  William Brohard

brohard design inc.
16045 jonella farm drive
purcellville, va 20132

CLIENT
  John's Incredible Pizza
DESIGN FIRM
  On The Edge Design
DESIGNERS
  Nicole Geiger-Brown, Jeff Gasper

110 Union Street
Suite 210
Seattle, Washington 98101

206 341 9885 phone
206 749 9868 fax

CLIENT
  Zaaz.com
DESIGN FIRM
  RMB Vivid, Inc.
DESIGNERS
  Brian Boram, Misha Zadeh

ZAAZ.com

unimobile.com

m

CLIENT
  Unimobile
DESIGN FIRM
  1185 Design
DESIGNERS
  Peggy Burke, Duane Reimer,
  Joan Takenaka, Garyle Brun,
  Rachel Fitzgibbon

2520 Mission College Boulevard, Suite 103, Santa Clara, California 95054, USA
tel › 408.969.8300   fax › 408.969.8324

523, 16th Main, III Block, Koramangala, Bangalore, 560 034, India
tel › 91.80.5521264   fax › 91.80.5531943

**Storage Way**

3501 West Warren Avenue | Fremont, California 94538
Tel: 510.360.5700 | Fax: 510.445.3522 | www.storageway.com

ZENERGY    16 MADRONA STREET ■ MILL VALLEY, CALIFORNIA 94941 ■ 415/380.ZMAX (9629)

**bluespring** | SOFTWARE

1128 Main Street, Third Floor
Cincinnati, Ohio 45210
513 794 1764 main
513 794 1724 fax
**www.bluespringsw.com**

CLIENT
Bluespring
DESIGN FIRM
Stein & Company
DESIGNERS
Stein Creative Team

**Pets Are Loving Support**

P.A.L.S.

*Help a friend keep a friend*

CLIENT
Pets Are Loving Support (P.A.L.S.)
DESIGN FIRM
Wages Design
DESIGNER
Elizabeth Sheehan

TEL 404.876.PALS
FAX 404.249.PETS
E-MAIL pals@palsatlanta.org

1058-C Northside Drive, Atlanta, Georgia 30318

CLIENT
Whole Health Pharmacy, Inc.
DESIGN FIRM
CommArts
DESIGNERS
Richard Foy, Keith Harley

ionis
INTERNATIONAL

CLEARSPRING PHARMACY, LTD.
201 UNIVERSITY BOULEVARD
DENVER · COLORADO · 80206
T 303 333 2010  F 303 333 2208
www.clearspringrx.com

4725 Quail Creek Lane    Boulder, CO 80301-3872 USA
Tel: 303 . 530 . 0680    800 . 571 . 8831    Fax: 303 . 530 . 0305
Email: contact@ionisinternational.com    Website: ionisinternational.com

CLIENT
Ionis International
DESIGN FIRM
Pollman Marketing  Arts, Inc.
DESIGNERS
Kevin Rogers, Jennifer Pollman

TELLURIDE FOUNDATION

charity

education

arts

athletics

618 Mountain Village Blvd. Suite 205 Telluride, CO 81435 **970 728 8717** fax 970 728 9007 www.telluridefoundation.org

CLIENT
 Telluride Foundation
DESIGN FIRM
 CommArts, Inc.
DESIGNER
 Mark Jasin

RDA

CLIENT
 RDA Corporation
DESIGN FIRM
 Crosby Marketing
 Communications
DESIGNER
 Ron Ordansa

CUSTOM SOFTWARE SOLUTIONS THAT MEAN BUSINESS

1966 GREENSPRING DRIVE SUITE 506 TIMONIUM, MD 21093 [800] 816.0333 [410] 561.9028 FAX [410] 561.9031 www.rdacustomsoftware.com

CLIENT
  The Streetview Group, Inc.
DESIGN FIRM
  Spare, Inc.
DESIGNER
  Richard Cassis

STREETVIEW GRP
unpedestrianMarketing

RYAN + ASSOCIATES

THE
STREETVIEW GROUP
INC

317.823.9515 VOX   10541 BARTLEY DR
317.823.9569 FAX   INDIANAPOLIS IN
                   46236

streetviewgroup.com

SPECIALISTS IN CONTRACT FURNISHINGS

8721 Pointe Drive • Broadview Heights, OH 44147
T: 440.838.1012 • F: 440.838.1541 • E: ryandassoc@aol.com

CLIENT
  Ryan & Associates
DESIGN FIRM
  Design Room
DESIGNERS
  Chad Gordon, Kevin Rathge

peak xv networks

corporate headquarters  2527 camino ramon suite 340 san ramon ca 94583  tel 925 468 7500  fax 925 242 7414  www.peakxv.net

returns online

Returns Online, Inc.

Island Corporate Center
Suite 650
7525 S.E. 24th Street
Mercer Island, WA 98040

(206) 230 - 8000 office
(206) 230 - 8003 facsimile
www.returnsonline.com

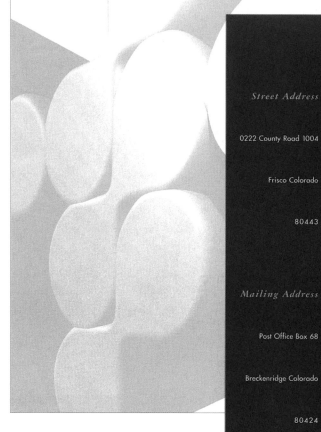

**sharemedia**
@ your service™

CLIENT
  Share Media
DESIGN FIRM
  Tim Kenney Design Partners
DESIGNERS
  Jamie Stockie, John Bowen

*Street Address*

0222 County Road 1004

Frisco Colorado

80443

*Mailing Address*

Post Office Box 68

Breckenridge Colorado

80424

*Telephone*

970 668 0999

*Facsimile*

970 668 4165

SUMMIT**STAGE**

ENVIRONMENT

CLIENT
  Summit County, Colorado
DESIGN FIRM
  Noble Erickson Inc.
DESIGNERS
  Jackie Noble, Steven Erickson,
  Robin Ridley

BELL DENTAL

855 NORTH CAHUENGA BLVD
HOLLYWOOD, CALIFORNIA 90038

323.460.4115 FX/323.460.6876

WWW.ANDERSONPRINTING.COM

Bell Dental Products, LLC
3003 Arapahoe Street #101B / Denver, Colorado 80205 / Tel: 303 292.2137 / Fax: 303 292.4411 / www.belldental.com

CLIENT
  Voyant Technologies
DESIGN FIRM
  Rassman Design
DESIGNERS
  John Rassman, Glen Hobbs

**voyant**

Voyant Technologies Inc.   1499 West 121st Avenue
Westminster, CO 80234-2076 USA   888.447.1087
303.223.5000   www.voyanttech.com

**gigabeat™**

950 Kifer Road · Sunnyvale · California · 94086 · P. 408 737-6120 · F. 408 737-6128

**gigabeat™**

AARON SCURLOCK
Finance
aaron@gigabeat.com

950 Kifer Road
Sunnyvale · California · 94086

P. 408 737-6120

F. 408 737-6128

C. 650 346-7603

CLIENT
  Gigabeat
DESIGN FIRM
  1185 Design
DESIGNERS
  Peggy Burke, Shannon Favata

**health** science

COMMUNICATIONS

16 West 22nd Street
New York, New York 10010
Tel: 212.462.4044
Fax: 212.741.7728
Internet: http://www.hsci.com

AN OMNICOM COMPANY

CLIENT
    Health Science Communications, Inc.
DESIGN FIRM
    Health Science Communications, Inc.
DESIGNER
    Robert Padovano

# HANDLER DESIGN GROUP INC

**17 RALPH AVENUE    WHITE PLAINS    10606**
**PHONE:  914 997 7592    FAX:  914 997 6467**

**www.handlerdesign.com**

CLIENT
    Handler Design Group, Inc.
DESIGN FIRM
    Handler Design Group, Inc.
DESIGNERS
    Bruce Handler

CLIENT
    Vastera
DESIGN FIRM
    Grafik Marketing Communications
DESIGNER
    David Collins

Opening the world to e-business

VASTERA

2111 Palomar Airport Road  Suite 250  Carlsbad CA  92009  ☎ 760.602.2900  ☎ 760.602.2910  www.kinzan.com

CLIENT
    Kinzan
DESIGN FIRM
    Visual Asylum
DESIGNERS
    Amy Jo Levine, MaeLin Levine,
    Gabriela Ramirez

CLIENT
  Explorica
DESIGN FIRM
  Corey McPherson Nash
DESIGNER
  Timea Adrian

←exɒlorica→

Explorica, Inc.
145 Tremont Street, 6th fl.
Boston, MA 02111
tel: 1.888.310.7120
fax: 1.888.310.7088

explorica.com

peoplebusinessnetwork™

People working better.

>www.peoplebusinessnetwork.com

CLIENT
  People Business Network
DESIGN FIRM
  C & A
DESIGNER
  Ken Thorlton

CLIENT
    Galerkin Design & Manufacturing
DESIGN FIRM
    Arkkit - Forms Design
DESIGNER
    David Mocarski

galerkin DESIGN & MANUFACTURING

Metropolitan Hotel

-769-1275   fax: 310-769-1155

569 Lexington Avenue, New York, NY 10022 • phone 800.METRO-NY • fax 212.758.6311

CLIENT
    Metropolitan Hotel
DESIGN FIRM
    Ziccardi & Partners
DESIGNERS
    Tracy Brennan, Nassos Gnafkis

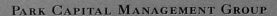

PARK CAPITAL MANAGEMENT GROUP

fax 615 370.0509
www.parkcapitalmanagement.com

970·266·8746  •  1015 WEST HORSETOOTH ROAD #111  •  FORT COLLINS, COLORADO 80526

BALDYGA GROUP
INTERNATIONAL, LLC

AN ENTERTAINMENT ORGANIZATION
1909 SOARING COURT  LAS VEGAS, NV 89134
T 702.256.3324  F 702.256.1324

CLIENT
    Baldyga Group
DESIGN FIRM
    Creative Dynamics, Inc.
DESIGNERS
    Victor Rodriguez, Christopher Smith

Rocky Mountain
ANGLERS

ROCKY MOUNTAIN ANGLERS, INC.
2539 Pearl Street
Boulder, Colorado 80302

Telephone: 303.447.2400  Facsimile: 303.447.2444  Email: rkymtanglr@aol.com

CLIENT
    Rocky Mt. Anglers
DESIGN FIRM
    Pollman Marketing Arts, Inc.
DESIGNER
    Jennifer Pollman

po box 772 redwood valley ca 95470  707.485.1083  fax:485.7726  www.degrassi.com  info@degrassi.com

TROPO
RECORDS

CLIENT
  Tropo Records
DESIGN FIRM
  Aufuldish & Warinner
DESIGNERS
  Bob Aufuldish, Kathy Warinner

DORSKY HODGSON + PARTNERS
SANDY SILVERMAN AIA    *Managing Principal, Washington DC*

*Architecture*
*Planning*
*Interiors*

1250 24th Street, NW
Suite 300
Washington, DC 20037

T 202.776.7733
F 202.776.7767
www.dorskyhodgson.com    CLEVELAND   FORT LAUDERDALE   WASHINGTON DC

CLIENT
  Dorsky Hodgson & Partners Inc.
DESIGN FIRM
  Epstein Design Partners
DESIGNER
  Maria Gutzwiller

**PORTICO**
CHERRY CREEK

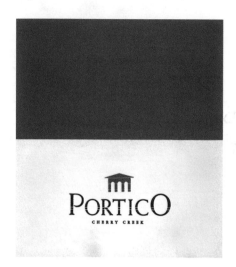

155-B FILLMORE STREET
DENVER COLORADO 80206
303.758.7611 FAX 303.377.4733

CLIENT
  Kestrel Partners
DESIGN FIRM
  Ellen Bruss Design
DESIGNERS
  Ellen Bruss, Charles Carpenter

amaze DESIGN, INC.
exhibit design

77 north washington street
boston massachusetts 02114
t:617.367.6300  f:617.742.8722

www.amazedesign.com

CLIENT
  Amaze Design
DESIGN FIRM
  Amaze Design
DESIGNER
  Kimberly Glyder

CLIENT
   Defteling Design
DESIGN FIRM
   Defteling Design
DESIGNER
   Alex Wijnen

**2448 EMERALD**
**EUGENE, OR 97403**

**ALEX WIJNEN**

**2448 EMERALD**
**EUGENE, OR 97403**
**TEL/FAX: 541.484.5392**
**EMAIL: defteling@hotmail.com**

**2448 EMERALD**
**EUGENE, OR 97403**
**TEL/FAX: 541.484.5392**
**EMAIL: defteling@hotmail.com**

**SpringDot**™
ENERGIZED
COMMUNICATION

**www.springdot.com**

2611 Colerain Avenue

Cincinnati, Ohio 45214-1711

tel. **513.542.4000**

fax. 513.542.4741

CLIENT
   Springdot
DESIGN FIRM
   Lipson Alport Glass & Assoc.
DESIGNERS
   Jon Shapiro, Mike Skrzelowski,
   Kevin Wimmer

Bellwether Solutions
25745 SE 34th Street
Sammamish, Washington 98075

Tel 425.837.9951
Fax 425.837.1623
www.bellwethersolutions.com

CLIENT
  Bellwether Solutions
DESIGN FIRM
  Dietz Design Co.
DESIGNERS
  Jin Kwon, Robert Dietz

TUMBLEWEED COMMUNICATIONS

CLIENT
  Tumbleweed Communications
DESIGN FIRM
  Cahan & Associates
DESIGNERS
  Bob Dinetz, Bill Cahan

Tumbleweed Communications GmbH,  Elsenheimer Straße 50, D-80687 München  T +49 (0) 89.58098.420  F +49 (0) 89.58098.425  www.tumbleweed.com

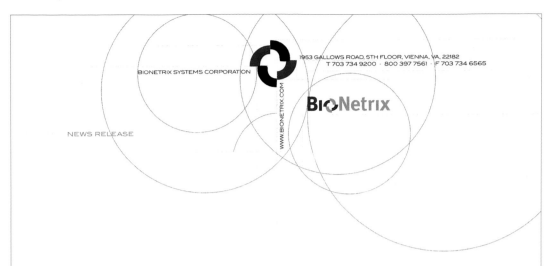

BIONETRIX SYSTEMS CORPORATION

1953 GALLOWS ROAD, 5TH FLOOR, VIENNA, VA, 22182
T 703 734 9200 · 800 397 7561 · F 703 734 6565

WWW.BIONETRIX.COM

**BioNetrix**

NEWS RELEASE

CLIENT
  Bionetrix
DESIGN FIRM
  Grafik Marketing Communications
DESIGNERS
  Franziska Güenther, Judy Kirpich,
  Kristin Moore, Lynn Umemoto

DANCE
CLEVELAND

CLIENT
  Dance Cleveland
DESIGN FIRM
  Epstein Design Partners
DESIGNER
  Brian Jasinski

1148 Euclid Avenue | Suite 311 | Cleveland . Ohio | 44115 | p. 216.861.2213 | f. 216.687.0022 | www.dancecleveland.org

CLIENT
    Women's Medical &
    Diagnostic Center
DESIGN FIRM
    Handler Design Group, Inc.
DESIGNER
    Bruce Handler

## Women's Medical & Diagnostic Center
An affiliate of IntegraMed America

Morris Notelovitz, MD, PhD
*Medical Director*

352/372-5600  Fax 352/376-3716

Floral Design

Event Consulting

26 West Braddock Road

Alexandria, VA 22301

Phone 703.739.9155

Fax 703.739.9045

www.Dragonfly-Floral.com

CLIENT
    Dragonfly
DESIGN FIRM
    Gibson Creative
DESIGNER
    Catherine Nunn

**Milwaukee County War Memorial**

*Phone:
/50 *

CLIENT
Milwaukee County War Memorial
DESIGN FIRM
Steve Horvath Design, Inc.
DESIGNERS
Steve Horvath, Peter Dombrowski

**m<sup>b</sup>**

**mission bay**

*A Catellus Urban Development Project*   255 Channel Street   San Francisco, California 94107   T 415 974-3737   F 415 974-3724   www.missionbaysf.com

CLIENT
Catellus Development Corporation
DESIGN FIRM
Muhlhauser & Young
DESIGNERS
Barbara Muhlhauser,
Lindsay Barth

# CORPORATE IDENTITY MANUALS

# typography

**U**se the Helvetica Neue fonts shown below for all copy except for names of Family and Friends of Barbie® Specific, main signage graphic lock-ups have been created and are shown in this guide and included on the CD. For other, supporting, in-store signage, mix and match a few of these fonts as shown below to create a fun, energetic style.

Each day is a *sunny* bouquet...
with **Flower Pretty™ Fashions!**

Collect them all!

*Helvetica Neue 43 Light Extended*
ABCDEFGHIJKLMNOPQRSTUVWX
YZabcdefghijklmnopqrstuvwxyz

*Helvetica Neue 47 Light Condensed*
ABCDEFGHIJKLMNOPQRSTUVWXYZabcdefghijkl
mnopqrstuvwxyz

*Helvetica Neue 57 Regular Condensed*
ABCDEFGHIJKLMNOPQRSTUVWXYZabcdefghijk
lmnopqrstuvwxyz

*Helvetica Neue 63 Medium Extended*
ABCDEFGHIJKLMNOPQRSTUV
WXYZabcdefghijklmnopqrstu
vwxyz

*Helvetica Neue 67 Medium Condensed*
ABCDEFGHIJKLMNOPQRSTUVWXYZabcdefghi
jklmnopqrstuvwxyz

*Helvetica Neue 73 Bold Extended*
ABCDEFGHIJKLMNOPQRSTUV
WXYZabcdefghijklmnopqrstu
wxyz

*Helvetica Neue 77 Bold Condensed*
ABCDEFGHIJKLMNOPQRSTUVWXYZabcdefghi
jklmnopqrstuvwxyz

*Helvetica Neue 93 Black Extended*
ABCDEFGHIJKLMNOPQRSTU
VWXYZabcdefghijklmnopqrs
tuvwxyz

*Helvetica Neue 97 Black Condensed*
ABCDEFGHIJKLMNOPQRSTUVWXYZa
bcdefghijklmnopqrstuvwxyz

*Barbie*

CLIENT
Mattel
DESIGN FIRM
Hamagami/Carroll & Assoc.
DESIGNER
Barbara Odza

ESSEX LOGO

SIGNATURE STAGING

Staging refers to the area directly surrounding the corporate logo. To ensure its visibility and integrity, the Essex Property Trust, Inc. signature staging area must be clear of other elements such as type, images, or other signatures.

# ESSEX
### PROPERTY TRUST, INC.

①
CLEARSPACE
The clearspace surrounding all
sides of the signature for all
applications is determined as the
distance from the top of the
signature to the underline.

CLIENT
Essex Property Trust, Inc.
DESIGN FIRM
Brad Terres Design
DESIGNERS
Brad Terres, Alan Blaustein

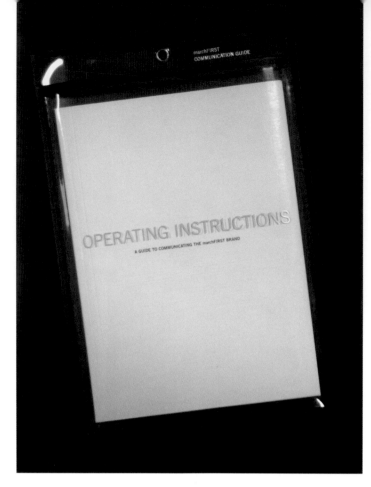

CLIENT
    marchFIRST
DESIGN FIRM
    VSA Partners, Inc.
DESIGNERS
    Adam Moroschan, Rachael Middleton,
    Ashley Wasem

CLIENT
    Simplex
DESIGN FIRM
    Bodzioch Design
DESIGNERS
    Leon Bodzioch, Richard May

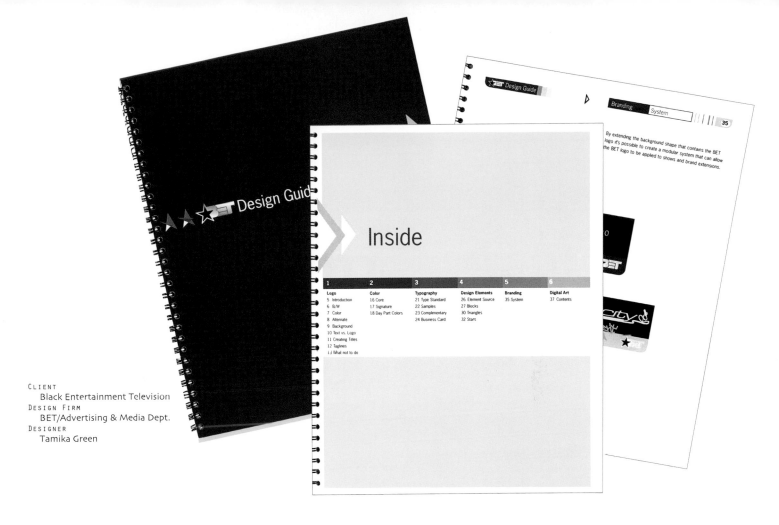

**CLIENT**
Black Entertainment Television
**DESIGN FIRM**
BET/Advertising & Media Dept.
**DESIGNER**
Tamika Green

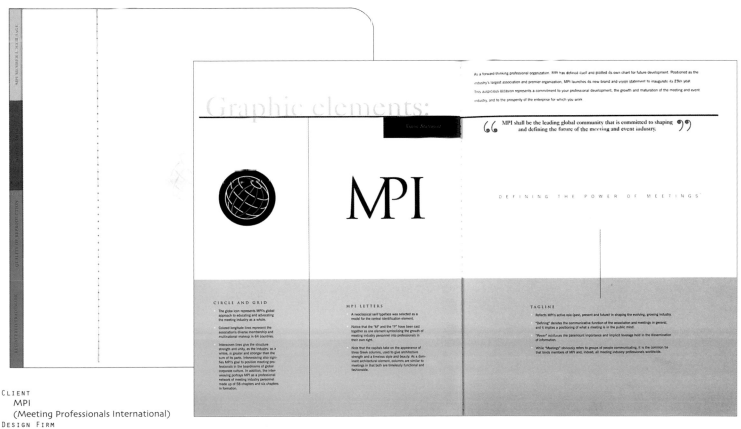

**CLIENT**
MPI
(Meeting Professionals International)
**DESIGN FIRM**
Peterson & Company
**DESIGNER**
Nhan T. Pham

2.1 The Signature

Shown here is the only approved signature format for City Harvest, Inc. The signature is composed of the logotype, support logotype and sub-graphic. The signature elements must be used together exactly as they appear on reproduction sheets and in digital files. Do not create new signatures for other entities, programs or services, etc.

• DO NOT MODIFY OR ALTER ANY SIGNATURE ELEMENTS.

**Logotype:** The logotype is a custom rendered typeface used for the City Harvest name.

**Support Logotype:** The support logotype is a custom rendered typeface used for the message "Rescuing Food For New York's Hungry".

**Sub-graphic:** The sub-graphic is a graphic rendering combining City Harvest's initials, an apple and a heart. The sub-graphic should not be separated from the logotype.

**Registered Trademark Symbol:** Always size and position the registered trademark symbol in proportion with size of the signature being used. Do not use the registered trademark symbol on signatures smaller than 1" in width.

REGISTERED TRADEMARK SYMBOL IS NOT ALWAYS REQUIRED; CONSULT ELLEN RUDLEY, DIRECTOR OF DEVELOMENT AND COMMUNICATIONS AT CITY HARVEST FOR USAGE GUIDELINES.

05.22.00

Basic Standards
the SIGNATURE **2.1**

CLIENT
  City Harvest
DESIGN FIRM
  Russell Design Associates
DESIGNER
  Tina Winey

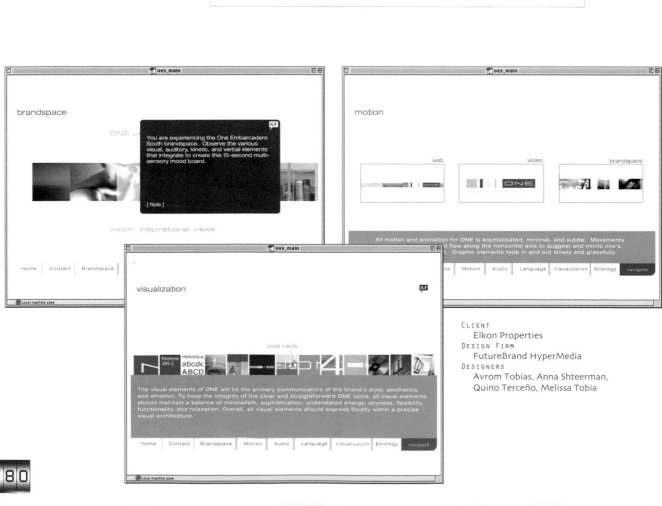

CLIENT
  Elkon Properties
DESIGN FIRM
  FutureBrand HyperMedia
DESIGNERS
  Avrom Tobias, Anna Shteerman,
  Quino Terceño, Melissa Tobia

CLIENT
University of Chicago
Graduate School of Business
DESIGN FIRM
Crosby Associates Inc.
DESIGNERS
Bart Crosby, Malgorzata Sobus,
Whitney Waters

CHICAGO ▦ GSB

Identification
and
Graphic
Standards

March 1, 2000  This program of identification and branding is the result of in-depth research and planning. It...

The University of Chicago Graduate School...

## The Wordmark

The wordmark is the official visual identifier for the Graduate School of Business and should be displayed prominently on all print and electronic communications and signage. It does not replace the official name of the school (the University of Chicago Graduate School of Business), but is now the official visual/verbal "nickname" of the GSB. It is more visible and more memorable than the complete name and better serves to increase awareness of the school and to unify all communications. It replaces all prior logotypes and emblems used by the GSB.

The wordmark is composed of the word Chicago and the abbreviation GSB separated by a special version of the university shield. It may be reproduced in a variety of color combinations, illustrated below. All elements of the wordmark, including the shield, have been custom drawn and cannot be reproduced with standard type fonts. The wordmark should never be respaced or modified in any way. All reproductions of the wordmark should be made from approved electronic files or printed repro proofs available from the GSB Publications Office (773.702.7431).

CLIENT
Chicago Convention &
Tourism Bureau
DESIGN FIRM
Davis Harrison Dion
DESIGNERS
Bob Dion, Dave Paoletti

# CHICAGO
CONVENTION AND TOURISM BUREAU

## The Icons

1. The icons must be displayed with the 'CHICAGO' wordmark and, ideally including 'Convention and Tourism Bureau.'

2. The wordmark must be black whenever it is paired with an icon. The only exception is when it is reversed.

3. Always display the icon in full color, never use screens or halftones.

4. Icons should not be placed over photographs or highly textured backgrounds.

5. Remember to keep the spacing tight between the icon and the wordmark.

6. Pantone values supplied upon request.

## Minimum Sizes

Ideally, the wordmark should never appear less than 1.5" wide.

When it must be used less than 1.5", the CCTB name can be stacked. This is the ONLY instance.

## Using a Background with Icons

1. The wordmark with icons should generally be reversed out of black.

2. When paired with the icons, this is the only instance where the color of the wordmark may be altered (white only).

## One-color Icon Use

1. For black and white use, line art for each icon has been created. Black is the only color the line art may appear in.

2. Avoid halftones — refrain from using the color icons for one-color jobs.

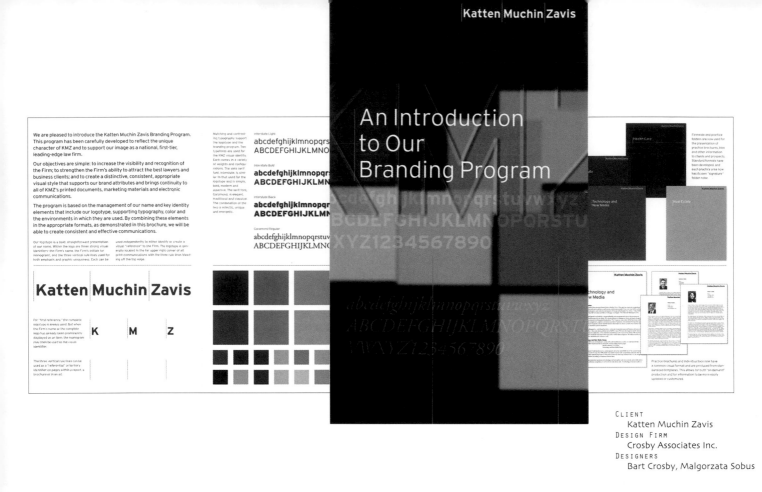

We are pleased to introduce the Katten Muchin Zavis Branding Program. This program has been carefully developed to reflect the unique character of KMZ and to support our image as a national, first-tier, leading-edge law firm.

Our objectives are simple: to increase the visibility and recognition of the Firm; to strengthen the Firm's ability to attract the best lawyers and business clients; and to create a distinctive, consistent, appropriate visual style that supports our brand attributes and brings continuity to all of KMZ's printed documents, marketing materials and electronic communications.

The program is based on the management of our name and key identity elements that include our logotype, supporting typography, color and the environments in which they are used. By combining these elements in the appropriate formats, as demonstrated in this brochure, we will be able to create consistent and effective communications.

## An Introduction to Our Branding Program

CLIENT
Katten Muchin Zavis
DESIGN FIRM
Crosby Associates Inc.
DESIGNERS
Bart Crosby, Malgorzata Sobus

CLIENT
DuPont
DESIGN FIRM
FutureBrand HyperMedia
DESIGNERS
Carol Wolf, Tom Li,
Thomas Nguy, Avrom Tobias, Sep Seyedi

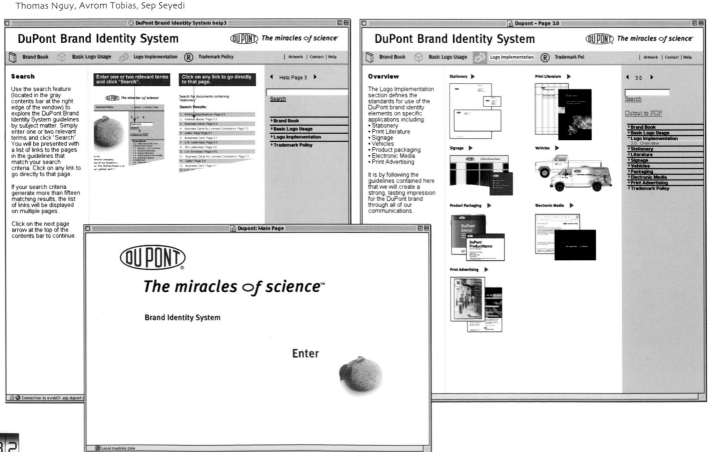

CLIENT
    Toys R Us/Animal Planet
DESIGN FIRM
    Alexander Isley Inc.
DESIGNERS
    Alexander Isley, Tara Benyei

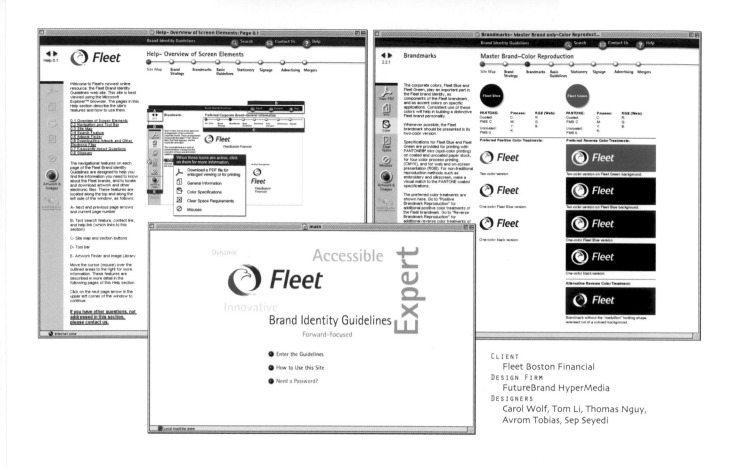

CLIENT
Fleet Boston Financial
DESIGN FIRM
FutureBrand HyperMedia
DESIGNERS
Carol Wolf, Tom Li, Thomas Nguy,
Avrom Tobias, Sep Seyedi

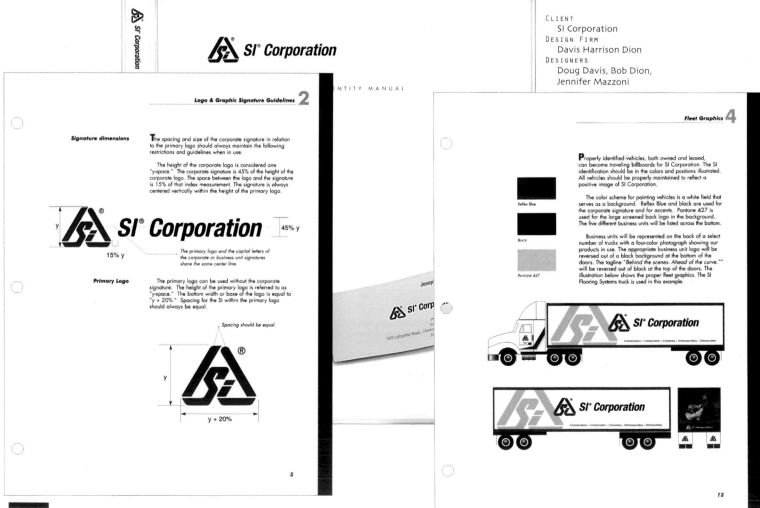

CLIENT
SI Corporation
DESIGN FIRM
Davis Harrison Dion
DESIGNERS
Doug Davis, Bob Dion,
Jennifer Mazzoni

CLIENT
  PNC Financial Services
DESIGN FIRM
  Cipriani Kremer Design
DESIGNERS
  Toni Bowerman,
  Jean Blundon

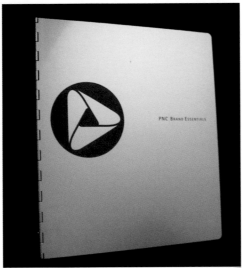

PNC BRAND ESSENTIALS

**3.3 The Brandmarks**

*Our brandmarks are the visual cornerstones of our brand identity. They are unique and proprietary, signifying the authenticity of our brand anywhere they appear. Our brandmarks symbolize the power and promise of PNC, representing the values we stand for. Because they are the visual expression of our identity, the following standards for implementing our brandmarks will ensure the integrity of a consistent, unified image.*

**3.3.1 Icon: PowerLink**

Our icon, the PNC PowerLink, with its integrated yet distinctive elements, is a visual translation of the dynamic power of integration. The abstract nature of its asymmetrical, geometric form connotes movement and energy as well as strength and stability. It is accessible, innovative, and reflective of our heritage. With its solid, steady footing, the PNC PowerLink provides a unifying element to all of our businesses. It depicts the coming together of separate entities, symbolizing that the sum is greater than the whole. Because the uniqueness of its design and association with PNC is essential, the PowerLink will provide brand recognition.

**Business Signatures**

The PNC businesses will adapt the PNC PowerLink icon and logotype into their names, in addition to incorporating the descriptor as a corporate endorsement. This will strengthen their ties to the PNC brand, enabling them to both contribute to and pull from the power and recognition of our new corporate identity. In order to distinguish the businesses as separate entities, each will have its own individual signature in the colors indicated below.

Specific artwork has been created for each business signature at large scale (any application 5" and above in height) and small scale (any application below 5" in height) in full color (spot color or CMYK), single color (black or PNC Platinum), and reverse options. Artwork also exists for these signatures with the corporate endorsement or the tagline. Never alter the artwork or substitute other versions of these signatures without the approval of Corporate Marketing.

| | | |
|---|---|---|
| PNC Blue<br>PNC Platinum | TOYO 0429<br>TOYO 1003 | PNCBANK |
| PNC Forest<br>PNC Platinum | TOYO 0904<br>TOYO 1003 | VentureBank@PNC |
| PNC Amethyst<br>PNC Platinum | TOYO 0950<br>TOYO 1003 | PNCAdvisors |
| PNC Platinum<br>PNC Onyx | TOYO 1003<br>TOYO Black | BlackRock |
| PNC Blue<br>PNC Platinum | TOYO 0429<br>TOYO 1003 | PNCMortgage |
| PNC Eggplant<br>PNC Platinum | TOYO 0961<br>TOYO 1003 | PNCRealEstateFinance |
| PNC Garnet<br>PNC Platinum | TOYO 0094<br>TOYO 1003 | PNCBusinessCredit |
| PNC Garnet<br>PNC Platinum | TOYO 0094<br>TOYO 1003 | PFPC |

**PNC AMETHYST**
TOYO    0950
CMYK    8/782/35/0
Web     102/51/153

| | PMS Coated | | PMS Uncoated |
|---|---|---|---|
| 30.12% | Rubine Red | 50.60% | Rubine Red |
| 27.01% | Process Blue | 43.50% | Phthalo Blue |
| 24.71% | Tint Base | 5.90% | Black |
| 18.16% | Black | | |

**PNC EGGPLANT**
TOYO    0961
CMYK    62/82/20/22
Web     102/51/102

| | PMS Coated | | PMS Uncoated |
|---|---|---|---|
| 34.42% | Tint Base | 64.40% | Rubine Red |
| 29.77% | Rubine Red | 31.60% | Reflex Blue |
| 22.09% | Reflex Blue | 2.60% | Black |
| 11.63% | Black | 1.40% | Yellow |
| 2.09% | Yellow | | |

**PNC ONYX**
TOYO    Black
CMYK    0/0/0/100
Web     0/0/0
        PMS Coated/Uncoated
100.0%  Black

# SIGNAGE/ ENVIRONMENTAL GRAPHICS

CLIENT
  Cherry Creek Shopping Center
DESIGN FIRM
  Ellen Bruss Design
DESIGNERS
  Ellen Bruss, Kara Cullen

CLIENT
  Reuters America Inc. and Instinct
DESIGN FIRM
  Edwin Schlossberg Inc.
DESIGNERS
  Edwin Schlossberg, Joe Mayer, Ron McBain,
  Dean Markosian, Mark Corral, Gideon D'Arcangelo,
  Angela Greene

CLIENT
  Envision Boulder
DESIGN FIRM
  Pollman Marketing Arts, Inc.
DESIGNER
  Jennifer Pollman

CLIENT
  Sound Transit
DESIGN FIRM
  Michael Courtney Design
DESIGNERS
  Mike Courtney, Dan Hoang

CLIENT
  Mitsui Fudosan
DESIGN FIRM
  RTKL Associates Inc./ID8
DESIGNERS
  RTKL Associates Inc./ID8

CLIENT
  Comerica Park/Detroit Tigers
DESIGN FIRM
  Kiku Obata & Company
DESIGNERS
  Kiku Obata, Laura McCanna, Chris Mueller, Jef Ebers,
  Teresa Norton-Young, Todd Mayberry, Amy Knopf,
  Carole Jerome, Gen Obata, Jennifer Baldwin, Jeff Rifkin,
  Heather Speckhard, Joe Floresca, Tim Wheeler

CLIENT
  Rocky Mountain Anglers
DESIGN FIRM
  Pollman Marketing Arts, Inc.
DESIGNER
  Jennifer Pollman

CLIENT
  Comcast Corporation
DESIGN FIRM
  Daroff Design Inc
DESIGNERS
  Karen Daroff, Alina Jakubski, Scott Winger,
  Martin Komitzky, Glen Swantak,
  Stephen Willison

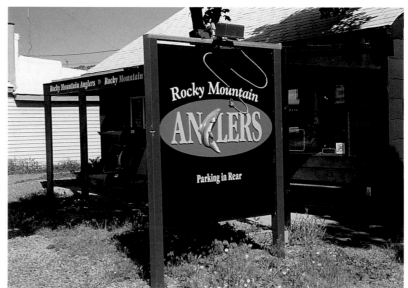

CLIENT
  The Cleveland Indians
DESIGN FIRM
  Herip Associates
DESIGNERS
  Walter Herip, John R. Menter

CLIENT
  Beaumont Hospital
DESIGN FIRM
  Ford & Earl Associates
DESIGNER
  Brian Tolly

CLIENT
  Time Warner
DESIGN FIRM
  Edwin Schlossberg Inc.
DESIGNERS
  Edwin Schlossberg, Diane Klein,
  Mary Niebauer, Matthew Moore, Angela Greene
  Dean Markosian, Ron McBain, Joe Mayer

CLIENT
  Dr. John J. Kicos, D.C.
DESIGN FIRM
  Performance Graphics
  of Lake Norman, Inc.
DESIGNER
  Mitzi Mayhew

CLIENT
  Spectra Securities
DESIGN FIRM
  Cullinane Design Inc.
DESIGNER
  Lynn Koble

CLIENT
  Hong Kong Land (Esplanade) Ltd.
DESIGN FIRM
  Calori & Vanden-Eynden
DESIGNERS
  David Vanden-Eynden, Gina DeBenedittis

CLIENT
  Chevron
DESIGN FIRM
  Addison
DESIGNERS
  Kraig Kessel, David Takeuchi,
  Arief Kartamihardja, Maria Wirjopranoto

CLIENT
  LookSmart
DESIGN FIRM
  Landkamer Partners
DESIGNERS
  Mark Landkamer, Kris Kargo

CLIENT
Verizon Communications
DESIGN FIRM
DeSola Group, Inc.
DESIGNERS
DeSola Group, Inc.

CLIENT
Pittsburgh Cultural Trust
DESIGN FIRM
Agnew Moyer Smith Inc.
DESIGNERS
Norm Goldberg, John Sotirakis,
Cat Zaccardi

CLIENT
Manny's Underground (Cafe)
DESIGN FIRM
Noble Erickson Inc.
DESIGNERS
Steven Erickson, Sarah Gandrud

CLIENT
   Nellis Air Force Base
DESIGN FIRM
   Creative Dynamics, Inc.
DESIGNERS
   Makenzie Walsh, Christopher Smith,
   Victor Rodriguez, Casey Corcoran

CLIENT
   The Pageant
DESIGN FIRM
   Kiku Obata & Company
DESIGNERS
   Kiku Obata, Kevin Flynn,
   Aia, Tom Kowalski, Jef Ebers

CLIENT
   Vulcan Northwest
DESIGN FIRM
   Michael Courtney Design
DESIGNERS
   Mike Courtney, Scott Souchock

CLIENT
Amtrak
DESIGN FIRM
Calori & Vanden-Eynden
DESIGNERS
David Vanden-Eynden,
Jordan Marcus, Denise Funaro

CLIENT
Teledesic
DESIGN FIRM
NBBJ Graphic Design
DESIGNERS
Brent Whiting, Tom Bender, Lara Swimmer,
David Gulassa, Martin Signs

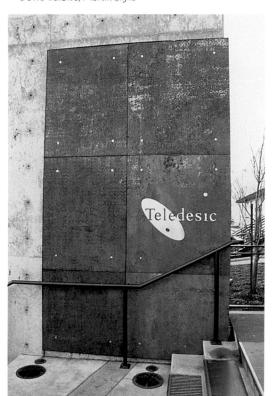

CLIENT
Taylor Made Golf Co.
DESIGN FIRM
Laura Coe Design Assoc.
DESIGNERS
Leanne Leveillee, Jenny Goddard, Ryoichi Yotsumoto,
Tom Richman, Laura Coe Wright

CLIENT
Audi of America
DESIGN FIRM
Design Forum
DESIGNERS
Scott Jeffrey, Amy Droll

CLIENT
Cherry Creek Shopping Center
DESIGN FIRM
Ellen Bruss Design
DESIGNERS
Ellen Bruss, Charles Carpenter

CLIENT
  Sunset Station Group
DESIGN FIRM
  Creative Link
DESIGNER
  Mark Broderick

CLIENT
  NBBJ Architects
DESIGN FIRM
  CommArts, Inc.
DESIGNERS
  Richard Foy, Dave Tweed

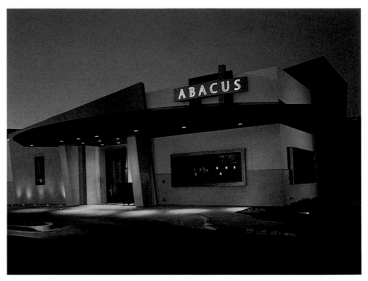

CLIENT
  LA Arena Company
DESIGN FIRM
  CommArts Inc.
DESIGNERS
  Richard Foy, Dave Tweed

CLIENT
  Empire Vision
DESIGN FIRM
  Shook
DESIGNERS
  Mike Nicolls, Ginger Riley,
  Linda Kratz, Cicley Worrell,
  Steve Fenton, Tim Buchman

CLIENT
  Abacus
DESIGN FIRM
  David Carter Design Associates
DESIGNER
  Steve Jordan

CLIENT
  Brixx
DESIGN FIRM
  Shook
DESIGNERS
  Mike Nicholls, Jeff Camillo,
  Wayne Morris

CLIENT
  Visual Asylum
DESIGN FIRM
  Visual Asylum
DESIGNERS
  Amy Jo Levine, MaeLin Levine

CLIENT
  University of Oregon
DESIGN FIRM
  Funk & Associates
DESIGNERS
  Chris Berner, Tim Jordan,
  Kathleen Heinz

CLIENT
  First Impressions
DESIGN FIRM
  Gold & Associates
DESIGNER
  Keith Gold

CLIENT
  NBBJ Architects
DESIGN FIRM
  CommArts, Inc.
DESIGNERS
  Richard Foy, Dave Tweed,
  Amy Schroeder

CLIENT
  Neoplan USA Corporation
DESIGN FIRM
  Noble Erickson Inc.
DESIGNERS
  Sarah Gandrud, Steven Erickson

CLIENT
  Clark Retail Enterprises, Inc.
DESIGN FIRM
  Addison
DESIGNERS
  Kraig Kessel, David Takeuchi, Nick Bently,
  Moe Suleiman, Arief Kartamihardja,
  Maria Wirjopranoto, Matt Versue

CLIENT
    The Mills Corp and Kan Am
DESIGN FIRM
    RTKL Associates Inc./ID8
DESIGNERS
    RTKL Associates Inc./ID8

CLIENT
    Bethesda Urban Partnership
DESIGN FIRM
    B+B Design
DESIGNER
    George Bird

CLIENT
    Southwestern Bell Corporation
DESIGN FIRM
    Fleishman-Hillard Design, St. Louis
DESIGNER
    Kevin Kampwerth

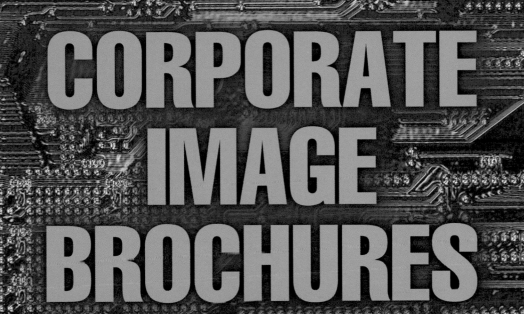

# CORPORATE IMAGE BROCHURES

CLIENT
    WellStar Health System
DESIGN FIRM
    WorldSTAR Design
DESIGNER
    Greg Guhl

CLIENT
    Beveridge & Diamond, PC
DESIGN FIRM
    Greenfield/Belser Ltd
DESIGNERS
    Burkey Belser, Charlyne Fabi

CLIENT
    The Museum Replica Gallery
DESIGN FIRM
    Carella And Company
DESIGNER
    Cliff Hall

CLIENT
    Stanley Associates
DESIGN FIRM
    Miravo Communications
DESIGNER
    Kanako Yamamoto

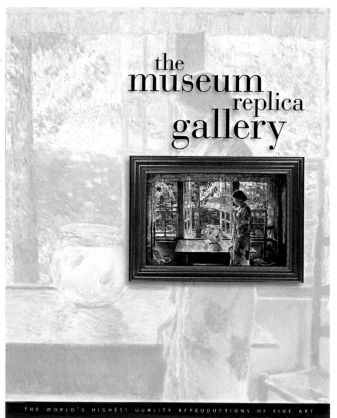

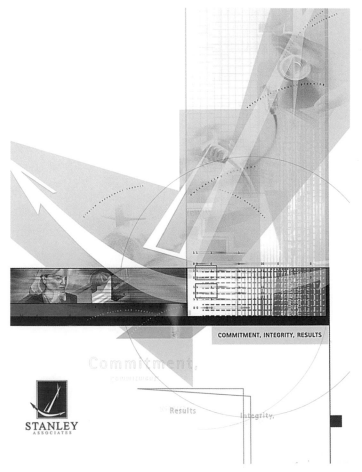

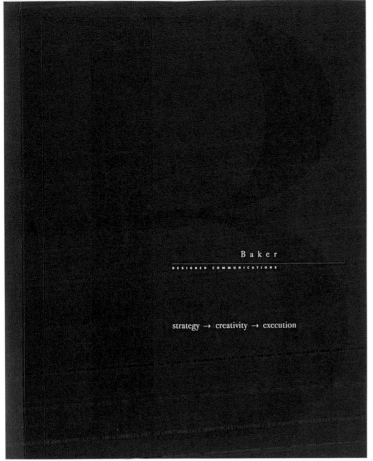

CLIENT
Baker Designed Communications
DESIGN FIRM
Baker Designed Communications
DESIGNERS
Gary Baker, Michelle Wolins

CLIENT
custom graphics, inc.
DESIGN FIRM
crawford design + associates
DESIGNER
Alison Crawford

CLIENT
Congressional Quarterly (CQ)
DESIGN FIRM
Kensington Creative
Worldwide, Inc.
DESIGNER
Donna Scofide Parrott

CLIENT
Steelcase Inc.
DESIGN FIRM
Genesis, Inc.
DESIGNERS
Jim Adler,
Beth Kreimer

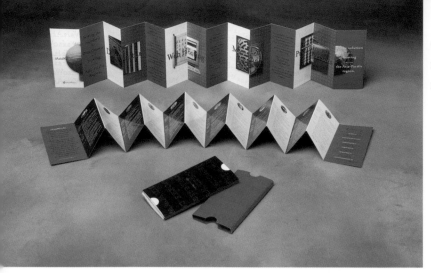

CLIENT
 iAsiaWorks, Inc.
DESIGN FIRM
 Gee + Chung Design
DESIGNERS
 Earl Gee, Fani Chung,
 Kay Wu, Kirk Amyx

CLIENT
 A to Z communications, inc.
DESIGN FIRM
 A to Z communications, inc.
DESIGNER
 Aimee Lazer

CLIENT
 Dam Creative
DESIGN FIRM
 Dam Creative

CLIENT
 Novell Inc.
DESIGN FIRM
 Hornall Anderson Design Works
DESIGNERS
 Larry Anderson, James Tee,
 Holly Craven, Michael Brugman,
 Kaye Farmer

HIGH-STAKES CASES

BUTTONED-DOWN, TEXAS STYLE   We hire the best and brightest graduates of the nation's leading
law schools and clerkship programs. But brains alone
don't make a trial lawyer. We teach our lawyers to
apply their brain power to real-life business and
courtroom challenges. The result: smart lawyers who
understand the business issues *and* can communicate
them to judges and juries.
 Carrington Coleman consistently ranks at the
TOP OF DALLAS LAW FIRMS in surveys
measuring academic achievement. Many of our
lawyers also served as law clerks to leading trial and
appellate judges in Texas and around the country—
giving us BEHIND-THE-SCENES EXPERIENCE
and valuable insights to help our clients.

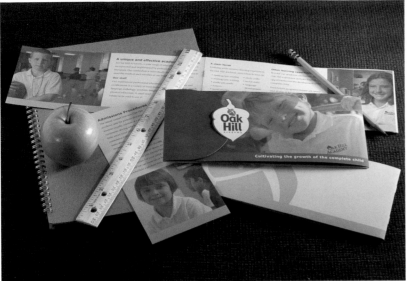

CLIENT
    Oak Hill Academy
DESIGN FIRM
    Dam Creative

CLIENT
    University of Colorado
DESIGN FIRM
    CommArts, Inc.
DESIGNER
    Keith Harley

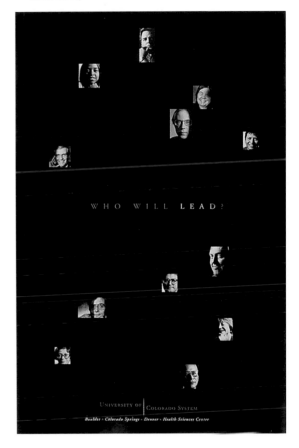

CLIENT
    Legendary Homes, Inc.
DESIGN FIRM
    The M. Group
DESIGNERS
    George Susich, Gary Miller

CLIENT
    Zunda Design Group
DESIGN FIRM
    Zunda Design Group
DESIGNERS
    Charles Zunda, Todd Nickel,
    Patrick Sullivan, Kelly Hopewell

CLIENT
  Charles Slert Associates Architects
DESIGN FIRM
  Nicholson Design
DESIGNERS
  Joe C. Nicholson, N. Charles Slert

CLIENT
  Triconex
DESIGN FIRM
  Strata-Media, Inc.
DESIGNERS
  Al Esquerra, Kimberly Hansen,
  Carrie Sandoval

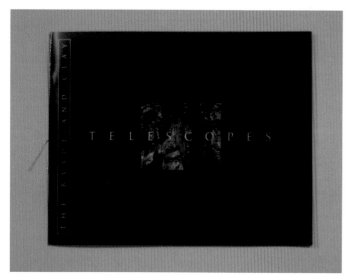

CLIENT
  Carnegie Institution of Washington
DESIGN FIRM
  Dieter Design
DESIGNER
  Maureen Dieter

CLIENT
  PG&E Energy Services
DESIGN FIRM
  Visigy
DESIGNERS
  Suzy Leung, Linda Kelly

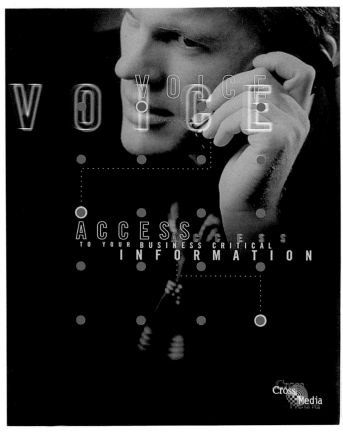

**CLIENT**
CrossMedia
**DESIGN FIRM**
EVD Advertising
**DESIGNER**
Marc Foelsch

**CLIENT**
Kayhan International
**DESIGN FIRM**
Melia Design Group
**DESIGNERS**
Mike Melia, Allan Orr,
Sven Oberstein

**CLIENT**
The LTC Group
**DESIGN FIRM**
The LTC Group/Liquid Graphix

**CLIENT**
North Pole
**DESIGN FIRM**
Cintara Corporation
**DESIGNER**
Terry Wetmore

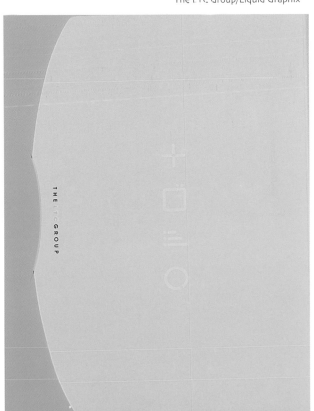

**Change is good.**

PLAZA **Cupertino**

| CUPERTINO, CALIFORNIA |

CLIENT
U.S. Advisor
DESIGN FIRM
Mastandrea Design, Inc.
DESIGNER
MaryAnne Mastandrea

CLIENT
The Richard E Jacobs Group
DESIGN FIRM
Herip Associates
DESIGNERS
Walter M. Herip,
John R. Menter, Sean P. Hunt

CLIENT
Carrington, Coleman, Sloman & Blumenthal, LLP
DESIGN FIRM
Greenfield/Belser Ltd.
DESIGNERS
Burkey Belser, Gloria Gullikson,
Gina Giaccardo

CLIENT
Blue Chair Design
DESIGN FIRM
Greenfield/Belser Ltd.
DESIGNERS
Burkey Belser, Stephanie Fernandez,
Tom Cauler

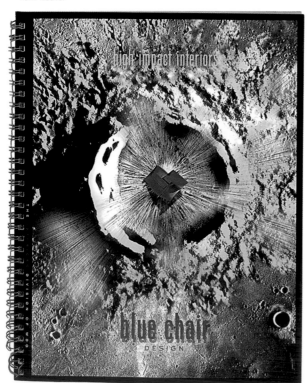

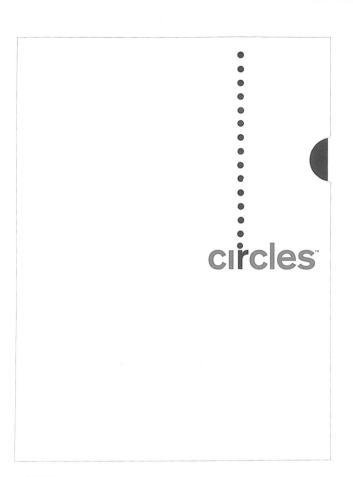

CLIENT
  The Printing Source, Inc.
DESIGN FIRM
  AKA Design, Inc.
DESIGNERS
  Craig Martin Simon,
  Richie Murphy

CLIENT
  Circles
DESIGN FIRM
  Corey McPherson Nash
DESIGNERS
  Michael McPherson,
  Rich Rose, Amy Esinfeld

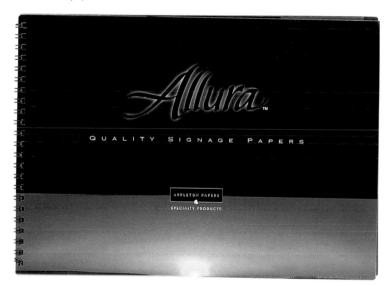

CLIENT
  Appleton Papers
DESIGN FIRM
  Directions Incorporated
DESIGNERS
  Chip Ryan, Lori Daun,
  Laura Timm

CLIENT
  Mobil Corporation
DESIGN FIRM
  Beveridge Seay Inc.
DESIGNERS
  Nick Seay, David Feinstein,
  Hubie Le

CLIENT
30sixty design, inc.
DESIGN FIRM
30sixty design, inc.
DESIGNER
Pär Larsson

CLIENT
Bluespring Software
DESIGN FIRM
Stein & Company
DESIGNERS
Stein Creative Team

CLIENT
Moore & Van Allen
DESIGN FIRM
Shook
DESIGNERS
Steve Fenton,
Ginger Riley

CLIENT
Seven Course Design
DESIGN FIRM
Graif Design
DESIGNER
Matt Graif

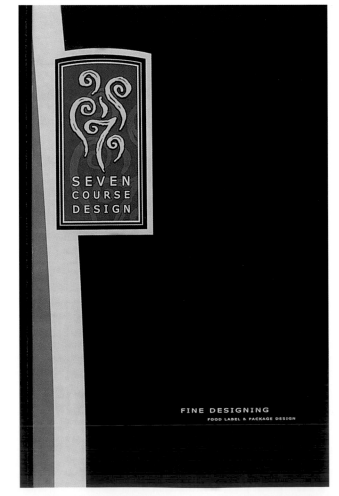

CLIENT
    KLS Professional Advisors Group Inc.
DESIGN FIRM
    Pisarkiewicz Mazur & Co. Inc.
DESIGNERS
    Linda Farber, Mary F. Pisarkiewicz

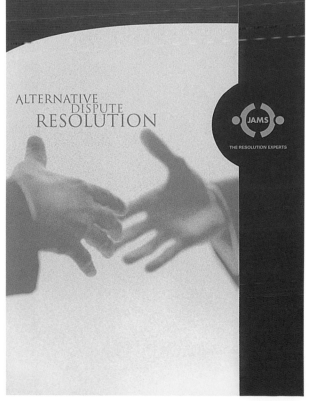

CLIENT
    The Richard E Jacobs Group
DESIGN FIRM
    Herip Associates
DESIGNERS
    Walter M. Herip,
    John R. Menter, Sean P. Hunt

CLIENT
    KDFC Radio Station
DESIGN FIRM
    Mastandrea Design, Inc.
DESIGNER
    Mary Anne Mastandrea

CLIENT
    JAMS
DESIGN FIRM
    Strata-Media, Inc.
DESIGNERS
    Al Esquerra, Robert Page

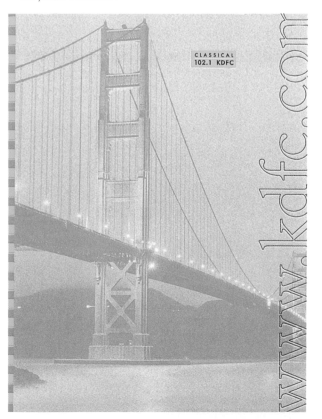

Celebrating
INDIVIDUALITY

CHANGE
MAKES YOU
VISIBLE

CLIENT
Rosewood Hotels & Resorts
DESIGN FIRM
David Carter Design Associates
DESIGNER
Sharon LeJeune

CLIENT
Methodologie
DESIGN FIRM
Methodologie, Inc.
DESIGNERS
Minh Nguyen, Claudia Meyer Newman

CLIENT
Contessa Food Products
DESIGN FIRM
BKD Design
DESIGNERS
Dave Matea, Jeff Barton

CLIENT
Kestrel Solutions
DESIGN FIRM
Visigy
DESIGNERS
Chelsea Hernandez, Linda Kelly

CONTESSA

CLIENT
Midwest Curtain Walls
DESIGN FIRM
Sheila Hart Design, Inc.
DESIGNER
Sheila Hart

CLIENT
Target Stores
DESIGN FIRM
Hedstrom/Blessing, Inc.
DESIGNER
Wendy LaBreche

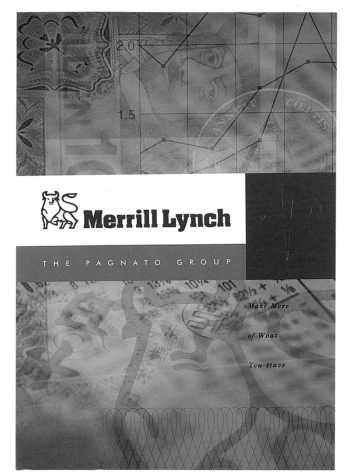

CLIENT
Merrill Lynch, The Pagnato Group
DESIGN FIRM
Smarteam Communications Inc.
DESIGNERS
Gary Ridley, Brent Almond,
Cade Martin, Linda Klinger

CLIENT
eJiva
DESIGN FIRM
A to Z communications, inc.
DESIGNERS
Aimee Lazer, Joe Tomko

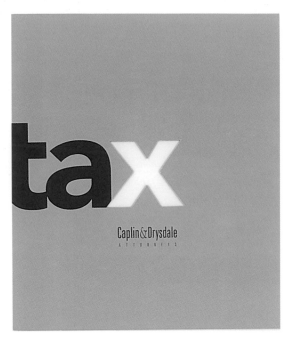

CLIENT
  Caplin & Drysdale
DESIGN FIRM
  Greenfield/Belser Ltd
DESIGNERS
  Burkey Belser, Gloria Gullikson

CLIENT
  Paramount Hotel Group
DESIGN FIRM
  Gouthier Design Inc.
DESIGNER
  Jonathan J. Gouthier

CLIENT
  VCampus
DESIGN FIRM
  EVD Advertising
DESIGNERS
  Tom Cosgrove, Krysta Higham,
  Heidi Fowler

CLIENT
  Green Bay Country Club
DESIGN FIRM
  Directions Incorporated
DESIGNERS
  Lori Daun, Chris Schudy

CLIENT
Ajunto
DESIGN FIRM
D4 Creative Group
DESIGNER
Wicky Wai-Kuen Lee

CLIENT
Fuze
DESIGN FIRM
Dietz Design Co.
DESIGNERS
Todd Karam, Robert Dietz

CLIENT
Hadassah
DESIGN FIRM
Hadassah Creative Services
DESIGNERS
Michael Cohen, Irit Hadari,
Julie Farkas

CLIENT
TJ Chameleon Design Communications
DESIGN FIRM
TJ Chameleon Design Communications
DESIGNER
Christopher Crawford

CLIENT
Visual Asylum
DESIGN FIRM
Visual Asylum
DESIGNER
Gabriela Ramirez

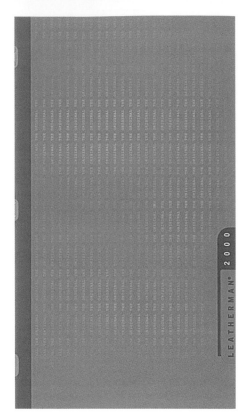

CLIENT
Leatherman Tool Group
DESIGN FIRM
Hornall Anderson Design Works
DESIGNERS
Jack Anderson, Lisa Cerveny,
Alan Florsheim, Don Stayner

CLIENT
Bay Area Jewish Healing Center
DESIGN FIRM
Bobby Reich-Patri Grafix
DESIGNER
Bobby Reich-Patri

CLIENT
Greater St. Louis Area Boy Scouts
DESIGN FIRM
Fleishman-Hillard Design, St. Louis
DESIGNERS
Kevin Kampwerth, Buck Smith

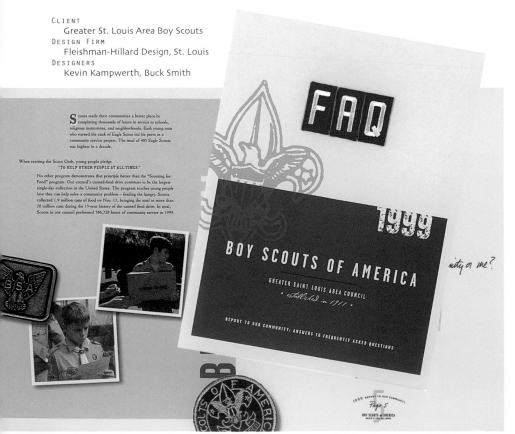

Healing happens...

CLIENT
  Simplex
DESIGN FIRM
  Bodzioch Design
DESIGNER
  Leon Bodzioch

**Cultivating the growth of the complete child**

CLIENT
  Oak Hill Academy
DESIGN FIRM
  DAM Creative Incorporated
DESIGNER
  Stephanie Elwick

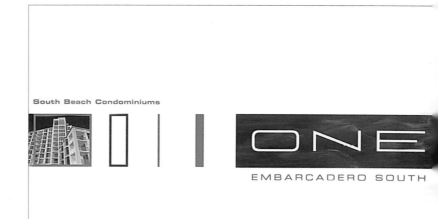

CLIENT
  Eikon Properties
DESIGN FIRM
  FurtureBrand HyperMedia
DESIGNERS
  Mario Natarelli, Anna Shteerman,
  Monse Miguell, Gabriela Jara

CLIENT
  Barnes Nursery Inc.
DESIGN FIRM
  Epstein Design Partners
DESIGNER
  Gina Linehan

CLIENT
  The Emerson Inn & Spa
DESIGN FIRM
  Carella & Company
DESIGNER
  Linda Kirkland

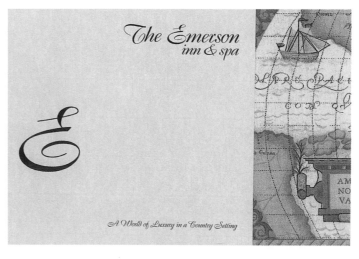

CLIENT
David Michael Miller Associates
DESIGN FIRM
Rowley Associates
DESIGNER
Jim Rowley

Brothers Concrete Construction, Inc.

CLIENT
Brothers Concrete Construction, Inc.
DESIGN FIRM
Lomangino Studio, Inc.
DESIGNER
Kim Pollock

CLIENT
SmartForce
DESIGN FIRM
Patt Mann Berry Design
DESIGNER
Patt Mann Berry

CLIENT
Bogart Golf
DESIGN FIRM
Hornall Anderson Design Works
DESIGNERS
Jack Anderson, James Tee,
Henry Yiu, Holly Craven, Mary Hermes

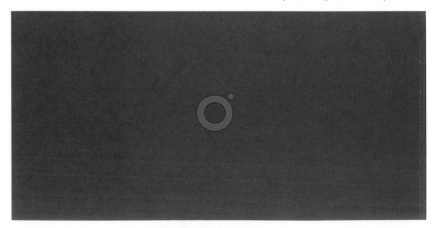

SmartForce 1999 Annual Report

**The Future is Open...**

Open source e-commerce solutions for real business.

akopia™

[i]e design

CLIENT
Akopia
DESIGN FIRM
Alpert & Alpert, Inc.
DESIGNER
Angela Buchanico

CLIENT
[i]e design
DESIGN FIRM
[i]e design
DESIGNER
Marcie Carson

CLIENT
Kestrel Solutions
DESIGN FIRM
Visigy
DESIGNER
Chelsea Hernandez

CLIENT
Vulcan Northwest
DESIGN FIRM
Michael Courtney Design
DESIGNERS
Mike Courtney, Scott Souchock

CLIENT
MPI (Meeting Professionals International)
DESIGN FIRM
Peterson & Company
DESIGNER
Nhan T. Pham

CLIENT
DAM Creative Incorporated
DESIGN FIRM
DAM Creative Incorporated
DESIGNERS
Matt Mollet, Stephanie Elwick

CLIENT
Door County
Chamber of Commerce
DESIGN FIRM
Directions Incorporated
DESIGNERS
Lori Daun, Chris Schudy

CLIENT
Visual Asylum
DESIGN FIRM
Visual Asylum
DESIGNER
Amy Jo Levine

"Discern the pattern and use it to your advantage."

Sun Tzu

InforMax®
High-Throughput Research™

CLIENT
InforMax, Inc.
DESIGN FIRM
Martin-Schaffer, Inc.
DESIGNER
Steve Cohn

CLIENT
Visual Asylum
DESIGN FIRM
Visual Asylum
DESIGNER
Joel Sotelo

CLIENT
Antec
DESIGN FIRM
Wages Design
DESIGNER
Matt Taylor

CLIENT
Visual Asylum
DESIGN FIRM
Visual Asylum
DESIGNERS
MaeLin Levine, Gabriela Ramirez

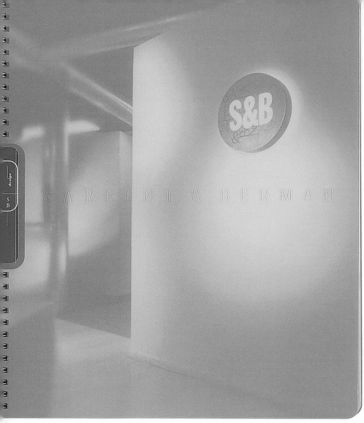

CLIENT
   Sargent & Berman
DESIGN FIRM
   Sargent & Berman
DESIGNERS
   Taleen Bedikian,
   David Vostmeyer

CLIENT
   Ocean Club
DESIGN FIRM
   David Carter Design Associates
DESIGNER
   Ashley B. Mattocks

CLIENT
   Idea Exchange
DESIGN FIRM
   The Moderns
DESIGNERS
   Sara Mears, Janine James

CLIENT
   Cintara Corporation
DESIGN FIRM
   Cintara Corporation
DESIGNER
   Terry Wetmore

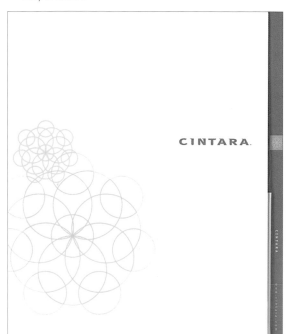

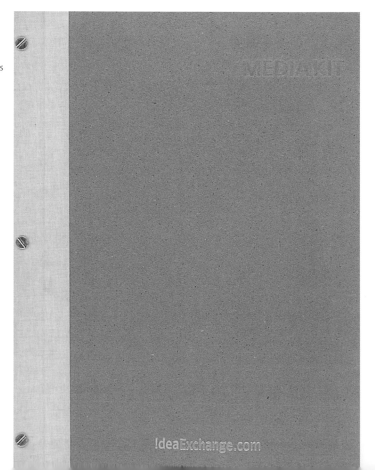

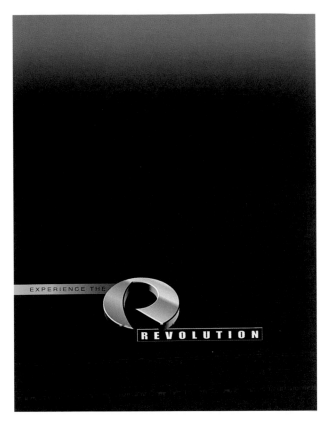

CLIENT
PCC Olofsson
DESIGN FIRM
Lord, Sullivan & Yoder
Marketing Communications
DESIGNERS
Axel Von Kaenel,
Kok Hwa Chung, Tracie Maye

CLIENT
Fraser Papers Inc.
DESIGN FIRM
Douglas Joseph Partners
DESIGNER
Scott Lambert

CLIENT
Dark Horse
Productions – GCEC
DESIGN FIRM
Kendall Creative Shop
DESIGNERS
Mark K. Platt, Tim Childress

CLIENT
LWO
DESIGN FIRM
Funk & Associates
DESIGNER
Alex Wijnen

GARDEN
FURNITURE

Elegant
outdoor
living that's
good for your
lifestyle
and the
environment

FSC

CLIENT
Hadassah
DESIGN FIRM
Hadassah Creative Services
DESIGNERS
Flinchum Inc., Michael Cohen

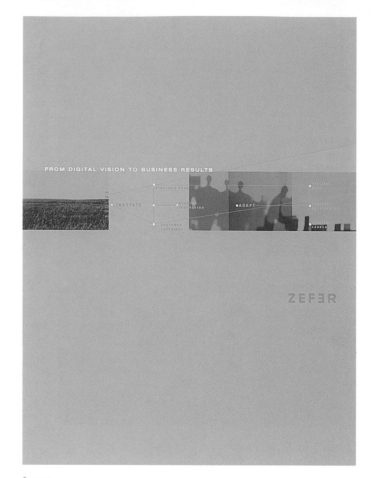

CLIENT
Zefer
DESIGN FIRM
Corey McPherson Nash
DESIGNERS
Phyllis Kido, Sarah Smith,
Zenobia Lakdawalla

CLIENT
marchFIRST
DESIGN FIRM
VSA Partners, Inc.
DESIGNERS
Dan Knuckey, Andrew Reeves

CLIENT
Coleman Spas
DESIGN FIRM
The M. Group
DESIGNER
Gary Miller

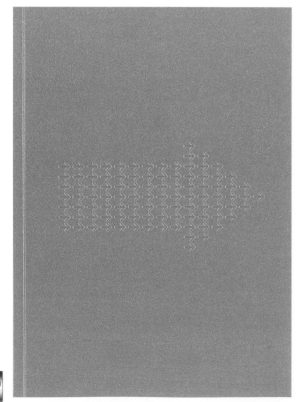

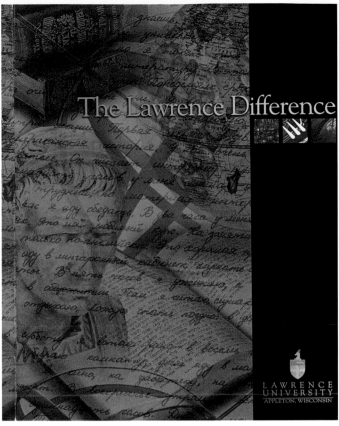

CLIENT
    Lawrence University
DESIGN FIRM
    Directions Incorporated
DESIGNERS
    Scott Mueller, Lori Daun,
    Chris Schudy

CLIENT
    Trefethen Vineyards
DESIGN FIRM
    Design Solutions
DESIGNER
    Deborah Mitchell

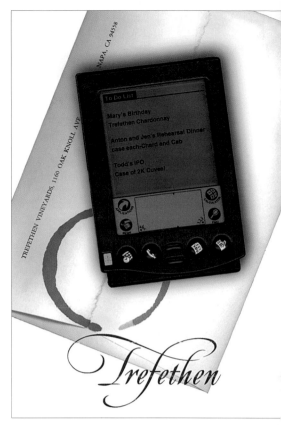

CLIENT
    PhotoZone
DESIGN FIRM
    Hornall Anderson Design Works
DESIGNERS
    Jack Anderson, Henry Yiu, Margaret Long,
    Rick Miller, Andrew Smith, Elmer Dela Cruz,
    Naomi Davidson

CLIENT
    Trefethen Vineyards
DESIGN FIRM
    Design Solutions
DESIGNER
    Deborah Mitchell

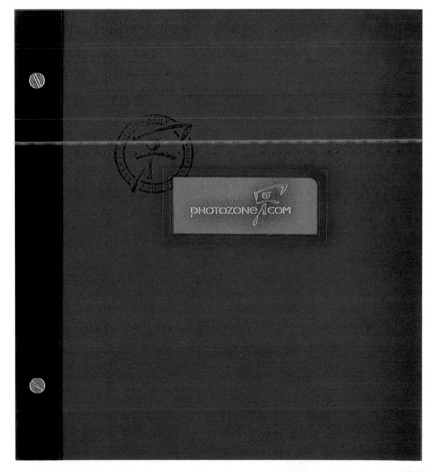

## The Queen Anne Way

*At Queen Anne Painting we paint every house as if it were our own. We use specific, exacting, proven methods to achieve painting excellence for your home.*

CLIENT
Tapestry in Time
DESIGN FIRM
Design Solutions
DESIGNER
Deborah Mitchell

CLIENT
Queen Anne Painting Co. Inc.
DESIGN FIRM
Gage Design
DESIGNER
Chris Roberts

CLIENT
The University of San Diego
DESIGN FIRM
Visual Asylum
DESIGNER
Rosa Torres

CLIENT
G&J Seiberlich & Co LLP
DESIGN FIRM
Design Solutions
DESIGNER
Deborah Mitchell

*Let His glory*

*fill the heavens.*

*Rejoice,*

*for He brings*

*love and peace*

*to the world.*

ALICE B. HAYES

Napa

St. Helena

Calistoga

Providing accounting and tax planning
services to the Napa Valley

CLIENT
Supon Design Group
DESIGN FIRM
Supon Design Group
DESIGNERS
Supon Phornirunlit,
Pum Mek-Aroonreung, Scott Boyer

CLIENT
Good Gracious
DESIGN FIRM
[i]e design
DESIGNER
Marcie Carson

CLIENT
Jillian's
DESIGN FIRM
On The Edge Design
DESIGNERS
Gina Mims, Jeff Gasper

CLIENT
Front Range
DESIGN FIRM
Hamagami/Carroll & Assoc.
DESIGNER
Jane Kim

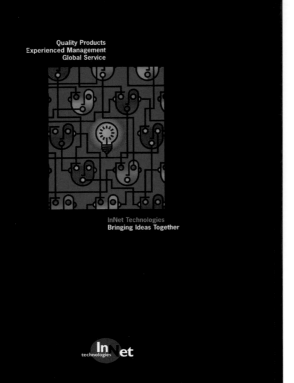

Quality Products
Experienced Management
Global Service

InNet Technologies
**Bringing Ideas Together**

InNet
technologies

CLIENT
InNet Technologies
DESIGN FIRM
Lorenz Advertising
DESIGNER
Arne Ratermanis

CLIENT
Brass Ring Systems
DESIGN FIRM
Visigy
DESIGNERS
Dan Liew, Chris Ardito

CLIENT
Robinson Knife Company
DESIGN FIRM
Michael Orr & Associates, Inc.
DESIGNERS
Michael R. Orr, Thomas Freeland

# TRADEMARK LOGO DESIGNS

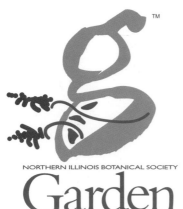

NORTHERN ILLINOIS BOTANICAL SOCIETY

## Garden Glory
Walk & Festival

CLIENT
Northern Illinois
Botanical Society
DESIGN FIRM
Anna Ohalla, Inc.
DESIGNER
Anna Ohalla

# FLAGSHIP
## UNIVERSITY℠

CLIENT
American Airlines
DESIGN FIRM
CS Creative
DESIGNERS
Cindy Slayton, John Evans

ITI
MARKETING, INC.

CLIENT
ITI Marketing Inc.
DESIGN FIRM
Gold & Associates
DESIGNERS
Keith Gold, Peter Butcavage

Terra Cotta
KITCHEN

CLIENT
Terra Cotta Kitchen
DESIGN FIRM
Power/Warner
Communications Group, Inc.
DESIGNER
Mark Poole

PEBBLE BEACH
1919
GOLF LINKS

CLIENT
Pebble Beach
DESIGN FIRM
Michael Schwab Studio
DESIGNER
Michael Schwab

DirtBanc.com

CLIENT
DirtBanc.com
DESIGN FIRM
AKA Design, Inc.
DESIGNER
Mike Mullen

CLIENT
Java Depot
DESIGN FIRM
Anna Ohalla, Inc.
DESIGNER
Anna Ohalla

CLIENT
The Pageant
DESIGN FIRM
Kiku Obata & Company
DESIGNER
Jennifer Baldwin

CLIENT
Black & Blu Entertainment
DESIGN FIRM
Zamboo
DESIGNER
Dave Zambotti

CLIENT
Mind Click Group
DESIGN FIRM
Zamboo
DESIGNER
Becca Bootes

CLIENT
The City of Louisville, KY
DESIGN FIRM
Kiku Obata & Company
DESIGNER
Rich Nelson

CLIENT
Alpha Omega Publications
DESIGN FIRM
The M. Group
DESIGNER
Meg Treon Coppersmith

cool strategies

CLIENT
Bass Hotels & Resorts
DESIGN FIRM
Degnen Associates, Inc.
DESIGNERS
Steve Degnen, Mark Denzer,
Dave Fowler

CLIENT
Cool Strategies
DESIGN FIRM
Strata-Media, Inc.
DESIGNERS
Dean Del Sesto, Lauren Ivy

sc magix

CLIENT
Scimagix
DESIGN FIRM
tompertdesign
DESIGNERS
Claudia Huber Tompert,
Michael Tompert

CLIENT
The Aviant Group
DESIGN FIRM
Jensen Design Assoc. Inc.
DESIGNERS
David Jensen, Jerome Calleja

CRMNOW

CLIENT
CRM Now
DESIGN FIRM
Strata-Media, Inc.
DESIGNERS
Al Esquerra, Robert Page

CLIENT
Medxcel
DESIGN FIRM
CS Creative
DESIGNER
Cindy Slayton

*the* LYLE & AILEEN WOODCOCK
museum At the center of
American Art and
Culture
St. Louis

CLIENT
Woodcock Foundation
DESIGN FIRM
Kiku Obata & Company
DESIGNERS
Kiku Obata, Jennifer Baldwin,
Tom Kowalski, Carole Jerome,
Teresa Norton-Young

CLIENT
Morris Building & Mgmt.
DESIGN FIRM
The M. Group
DESIGNER
Adair Payne

CLIENT
Wofex
DESIGN FIRM
Frankfurt Balkind Partners
DESIGNER
David Suh

CLIENT
New Frontier Bank
DESIGN FIRM
Kiku Obata & Company
DESIGNER
Joe Floresca

CLIENT
Ville Painters, Inc.
DESIGN FIRM
Albert/Bogner Design
DESIGNERS
Marie-Elaina Miller, Kelly Albert

CLIENT
Baton Records
DESIGN FIRM
Zamboo
DESIGNER
Dave Zambotti

CLIENT
Angela Jackson
DESIGN FIRM
Studio J
DESIGNER
Angela Jackson

# YOUTHSTREAM™
## MEDIA NETWORKS

# SUI GENERIS

CLIENT
Youth Stream
DESIGN FIRM
Frankfurt Balkind Partners
DESIGNER
David Suh

CLIENT
Sui Generis
DESIGN FIRM
Frankfurt Balkind Partners
DESIGNER
David Suh

# OPUS360

CLIENT
Opus 360
DESIGN FIRM
Frankfurt Balkind Partners
DESIGNER
David Suh

CLIENT
Circus Boys Comedy
DESIGN FIRM
Michael Niblett Design
DESIGNER
Michael Niblett

# ROBERT MONDAVI

CLIENT
Robert Mondavi
DESIGN FIRM
Michael Schwab Studio
DESIGNER
Michael Schwab

# S&K REALTY SERVICES, INC.

CLIENT
S&K Realty Services, Inc.
DESIGN FIRM
Bullet Communications, Inc.
DESIGNER
Timothy Scott Kump

CLIENT
Past Twelve
DESIGN FIRM
Tisha Lozano Design
DESIGNER
Michael Sanchez

CLIENT
Michael Tompert
DESIGNER
Michael Tompert

CLIENT
Eleven Acceleration, Inc.
DESIGN FIRM
Braley Design
DESIGNER
Michael Braley

CLIENT
Kovacs Gourmet Smokehouse
DESIGN FIRM
Hans Flink Design Inc.
DESIGNERS
Marilina Yang, Michael Troian

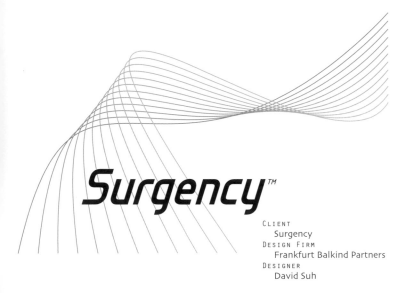

## Surgency™

CLIENT
Surgency
DESIGN FIRM
Frankfurt Balkind Partners
DESIGNER
David Suh

CLIENT
The Pageant
DESIGN FIRM
Kiku Obata & Company
DESIGNER
Rich Nelson

## resourcenet CAPITAL

CLIENT
ResourceNet Capital
DESIGN FIRM
Triad, Inc.
DESIGNER
Diana Kollanyi

## Barra

CLIENT
Barra
DESIGN FIRM
Addison
DESIGNER
Lindon Leader

CLIENT
Creative Management Coordinators
DESIGN FIRM
Zamboo
DESIGNERS
Becca Bootes, Dave Zambotti

 Poettker Construction

CLIENT
Poettker Construction
DESIGN FIRM
Stan Gellman Graphic Design Inc.
DESIGNERS
Barry Tilson, Erin Goter

CLIENT
  Manuel and Linda Herrera
DESIGN FIRM
  LoBue Creative
DESIGNER
  Gary LoBue, Jr.

CLIENT
  Nogginaut
DESIGN FIRM
  Nogginaut, Inc.
DESIGNER
  Julian Jackson

**nogginaut**

CLIENT
  Blaine Berger, Electronic Oasis
DESIGN FIRM
  Lightspeed Commercial Arts
DESIGNER
  Michael J. Hamers

CLIENT
  Esilicon
DESIGN FIRM
  Addison
DESIGNER
  David Schuemann

CLIENT
  MedEv ,LLC
DESIGN FIRM
  AKA Design, Inc.
DESIGNER
  Richie Murphy

CLIENT
  Quanta Piko
DESIGN FIRM
  Delphine Keim Campbell
DESIGNER
  Delphine Keim Campbell

CLIENT
Clark Retail Enterprises, Inc.
DESIGN FIRM
Addison
DESIGNERS
David Schuemann, Melton Castro,
Kartika Lie

CLIENT
Fuel Pizza
DESIGN FIRM
Shook
DESIGNERS
Jeff Camillo, Ginger Riley

THE MICHAEL J. | FOUNDATION FOR
FOX | PARKINSON'S
| RESEARCH

CLIENT
Michael J Fox Foundation
DESIGN FIRM
Frankfurt Balkind Partners
DESIGNERS
Kent Hunter, David Suh

CLIENT
Zfilmmaker
DESIGN FIRM
Zamboo
DESIGNER
Dave Zambotti

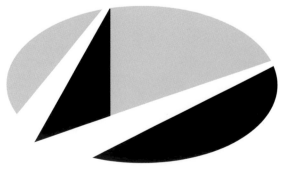

CLIENT
Veterinary Resource Group
DESIGN FIRM
Wirestone Colorado
DESIGNER
Bob Donovan

CLIENT
American Health Products
DESIGN FIRM
Identity Center
DESIGNERS
Wayne Kosterman, Tom Wilson

CLIENT
    St. Louis Zoo
DESIGN FIRM
    Kiku Obata & Company
DESIGNER
    Rich Nelson

**PHAROS OPTICS**

CLIENT
    Pharos Optics
DESIGN FIRM
    Zamboo
DESIGNER
    Becca Bootes

**MINERAL SPRINGS**

CLIENT
    Mineral Springs
DESIGN FIRM
    Peggy Lauritsen Design Group
DESIGNER
    John Haines

NetGenesis

CLIENT
    Deer Run Country Club
DESIGN FIRM
    Interbrand Hulefeld
DESIGNER
    Christian Neidhard

CLIENT
    NetGenesis
DESIGN FIRM
    Frankfurt Balkind Partners
DESIGNER
    David Suh

CLIENT
   IMS
DESIGN FIRM
   EHR Design
DESIGNERS
   Mark Rue, Daniel Sandboch

## GIANTLOOP
### NETWORK

CLIENT
   Giant Loop
DESIGN FIRM
   Corey McPherson Nash
DESIGNERS
   Phyllis Kido, Sarah Smith

CLIENT
   Premiere Dental Group
DESIGN FIRM
   Zamboo
DESIGNER
   Dave Zambotti

**ASPIRE**
EDUCATIONAL SERVICES

CLIENT
   Aspire Educational Services
DESIGN FIRM
   Jeff Fisher LogoMotives
DESIGNER
   Jeff Fisher

Tier
Expect A Lot

CLIENT
   Tier
DESIGN FIRM
   Triad, Inc.
DESIGNERS
   Diana Kollanyi, Cathy Danzeisen

### ›KNIGHT RIDDER›

CLIENT
   Knight Ridder
DESIGN FIRM
   Frankfurt Balkind Partners
DESIGNER
   David Suh

# SOMA SQUARE

CLIENT
Soma Square
DESIGN FIRM
Frankfurt Balkind Partners
DESIGNER
David Suh

# duet

CLIENT
Duet Incorporated
DESIGN FIRM
Beveridge Seay Inc.
DESIGNERS
Nick Seay, David Feinstein,
Marilia Costa

# About.com

CLIENT
About.com
DESIGN FIRM
Frankfurt Balkind Partners
DESIGNER
David Suh

# SANCTUM

CLIENT
Sanctum
DESIGN FIRM
Frankturt Balkind Partners
DESIGNERS
David Suh, Alfred Assin

# oasis

CLIENT
Oasis Gallery
DESIGN FIRM
Seran Design
DESIGNER
Sang Yoon

# Centerprise

CLIENT
Centerprise
DESIGN FIRM
Lipson Alport Glass & Assoc.
DESIGNER
Katherine Holderied

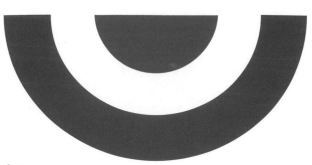

CLIENT
Alliance For Better Campaigns
DESIGN FIRM
Beveridge Seay Inc.
DESIGNERS
David Feinstein, Hubie Le,
Nick Seay

CLIENT
Bagel Bistro
DESIGN FIRM
Balderman Creative Services
DESIGNER
Bobbi Balderman

## Susan Marie & Associates
*Inspiration Coaching*

CLIENT
Susan Marie & Associates
DESIGN FIRM
Balderman Creative Services
DESIGNER
Bobbi Balderman

CLIENT
Gazelle Technologies
DESIGN FIRM
Zamboo
DESIGNER
Dave Zambotti

CLIENT
Disabled Children's Association
of Saudi Arabia
DESIGN FIRM
Beveridge Seay Inc.
DESIGNERS
Jack Beveridge, Nick Seay

CLIENT
4PointsTravel
DESIGN FIRM
Insight Design Communications
DESIGNERS
Tracy Holdeman, Sherrie Holdeman

DOGLOO®

*An Active Imagination™*

CLIENT
Dogloo
DESIGN FIRM
Zamboo
DESIGNER
Dave Zambotti

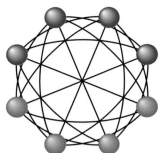

ALLEGIS
CAPITAL

CLIENT
Allegis Capital
DESIGN FIRM
Frankfurt Balkind Partners
DESIGNER
David Suh

mobile money℠

CLIENT
M2
DESIGN FIRM
Frankfurt Balkind Partners
DESIGNERS
David Suh, Lauren Adams

MONTEREY
HANDCRAFTED ★ ORGANIC
SODA™

CLIENT
Monterey Beverage Co.
DESIGN FIRM
Full Steam Marketing & Design
DESIGNER
Darryl Zimmerman

**Diesel Technology Forum**

CLIENT
Rowan & Blewitt Incorporated
DESIGN FIRM
Fleury Design
DESIGNER
Ellen Fleury

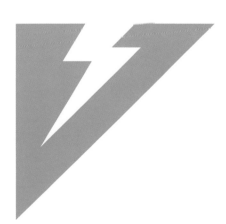

**Paradigm**

CLIENT
Paradigm Strategy Group, Inc.
DESIGN FIRM
Beveridge Seay Inc.
DESIGNER
Nick Seay

FireBoxx

CLIENT
Fireboxx/BD&L
DESIGN FIRM
TGD Communications
DESIGNERS
Gloria Vestal, Rochelle Gray

SpringDot™
ENERGIZED
COMMUNICATION

CLIENT
SpringDot
DESIGN FIRM
Lipson Alport Glass & Assoc.
DESIGNERS
Jon Shapiro, Kevin Winner,
Mike Skrzelowski

BLUE SEAS
FRESH SEAFOOD FROM SUSTAINABLE WATERS™

CLIENT
Genaurdi's Family Markets
DESIGN FIRM
Shook
DESIGNERS
Jeff Camillo, Ginger Riley

CLIENT
Alexander Dawson School-
Mascot Las Vegas
DESIGN FIRM
Ripple Strategic Design & Consulting
DESIGNERS
Laura Zollar, Raymond Perez

CHICAGO
CONVENTION AND TOURISM BUREAU

CHICAGO
CONVENTION AND TOURISM BUREAU

CLIENT
Chicago Convention & Tourism Bureau
DESIGN FIRM
Davis Harrison Dion
DESIGNERS
Bob Dion, Dave Paoletti

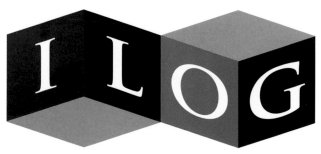

ILOG

CLIENT
ILOG
DESIGN FIRM
Landkamer Partners
DESIGNERS
Mark Landkamer, Gene Clark

# NORS™

**CLIENT**
Nors Sport
**DESIGN FIRM**
Jasper & Bridge
**DESIGNER**
Alexander Bridge

# GOAHEAD

**CLIENT**
GoAhead Software
**DESIGN FIRM**
Walsh & Associates, Inc.
**DESIGNERS**
Miriam Lisco

**CLIENT**
Sibling Systems
**DESIGN FIRM**
tompertdesign
**DESIGNERS**
Claudia Huber Tompert,
Michael Tompert

**CLIENT**
Steiner & Associates
**DESIGN FIRM**
Development Design Group
**DESIGNER**
Amanda Moreau

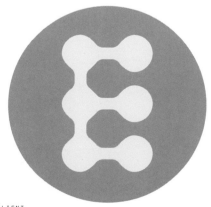

**CLIENT**
Element Group
**DESIGN FIRM**
Element Group
**DESIGNER**
Eric Mueller

**CLIENT**
IntegraTech Corporation
**DESIGN FIRM**
Gage Design
**DESIGNER**
Chris Roberts

CLIENT
Fresh Express
DESIGN FIRM
Full Steam Marketing & Design
DESIGNERS
Darryl Zimmerman, Gayle Kabaker

CLIENT
Bold Lions
Creative Arts Education
DESIGN FIRM
The Wecker Group
DESIGNERS
Robert Wecker, Tremayne Cryer

CLIENT
Ripple
DESIGN FIRM
Ripple Strategic Design & Consulting
DESIGNERS
Dan McElhattan III, Laura Zollar,
Raymond Perez

CLIENT
Verizon Communications
DESIGN FIRM
DeSola Group, Inc.
DESIGNERS
DeSola Group

GSM
GLOBAL NETWORK℠

CLIENT
Think New Ideas, Inc.
DESIGN FIRM
Zenn Graphic Design
DESIGNER
Zengo Yoshida

MIKA COLOR

CLIENT
Mika Color
DESIGN FIRM
Zenn Graphic Design
DESIGNER
Zengo Yoshida

CLIENT
Excel
DESIGN FIRM
Menefee & Partners and
Insight Design Communications
DESIGNERS
Tracy Holdeman, Sherrie Holdeman,
Greg Menefee, Paul Hanson

CLIENT
Excel
DESIGN FIRM
Menefee & Partners and
Insight Design Communications
DESIGNERS
Tracy Holdeman, Sherrie Holdeman,
Greg Menefee, Paul Hanson

# OBCTV.COM

CLIENT
OBCTV
DESIGN FIRM
After Hours Creative
DESIGNERS
After Hours Creative

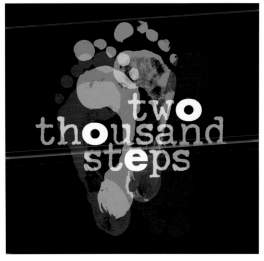

two
thousand
steps

CLIENT
Orange County Performing Arts Center
DESIGN FIRM
Hayden Design
DESIGNERS
Tricia Hayden, Robert Hayden

*Dayspring Farm*

CLIENT
Dayspring Farm
DESIGN FIRM
Walsh & Associates, Inc.
DESIGNERS
Miriam Lisco, Jim Hays,
Jane Shasky

# cyberstylist*

CLIENT
Harrison Smith
DESIGNER
Brent Almond

**CLIENT**
Excel
**DESIGN FIRM**
Menefee & Partners and
Insight Design Communications
**DESIGNERS**
Tracy Holdeman, Sherrie Holdeman,
Greg Menefee, Paul Hanson

**CLIENT**
Smart Link Technologies, Ltd.
**DESIGN FIRM**
Stewart Monderer Design, Inc.
**DESIGNER**
Stewart Monderer

**BHERMAN** DEVELOPMENT

**CLIENT**
Bherman Development
**DESIGNER**
Brent Almond

**CONNECT A-DEAL**
MORTGAGE MAKERS

**CLIENT**
Connect-A-Deal Mortgage Makers
**DESIGN FIRM**
The Wecker Group
**DESIGNER**
Robert Wecker

KID'S JAM FOUNDATION

**CLIENT**
Kid's Jam Foundation
**DESIGN FIRM**
Ripple Strategic Design & Consulting
**DESIGNERS**
Dan McElhattan III,

**Crop Systems International**

**CLIENT**
Crop Systems International
**DESIGN FIRM**
Lorenz Advertising
**DESIGNER**
Arne Ratermanis

**ZAiQ** TECHNOLOGIES

**EndPoints**

**CLIENT**
Zaiq Technologies, Inc.
**DESIGN FIRM**
Stewart Monderer Design, Inc.
**DESIGNER**
Stewart Monderer

**CLIENT**
EndPoints, Inc.
**DESIGN FIRM**
Stewart Monderer Design, Inc.
**DESIGNERS**
Jason CK Miller, Stewart Monderer

CLIENT
Armeta
DESIGN FIRM
Kendall Creative Shop
DESIGNER
Mark K. Platt

CLIENT
Fabrichem Systems
DESIGN FIRM
Creative Dynamics, Inc.
DESIGNERS
Christopher Smith, Victor Rodriguez

CLIENT
Ultimate Marketing
DESIGN FIRM
The Wecker Group
DESIGNER
Robert Wecker

CLIENT
International Society For Optical
Engineering
DESIGN FIRM
GAF Adv Dsn
DESIGNER
Gregg Floyd

CLIENT
Vantage Eye Center
DESIGN FIRM
Full Steam Marketing & Design
DESIGNER
Liz Nolan

CLIENT
net@work/etronics
DESIGN FIRM
Zinzell
DESIGNER
Don Zinzell

CLIENT
Frank Lloyd Wright Preservation Trust
DESIGN FIRM
Liska + Associates, Inc.
DESIGNER
Anna Moore

CLIENT
Nuance
DESIGN FIRM
Landkamer Partners
DESIGNERS
Mark Landkamer, Gene Clark

*crafting the patterns of a meaningful life*℠

CLIENT
  The Bromley Companies
DESIGN FIRM
  Noble Erickson Inc.
DESIGNERS
  Jackie Noble, Robin Ridley

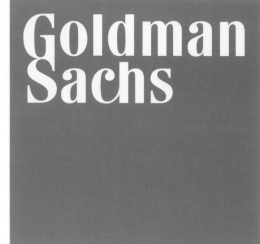

CLIENT
  Goldman Sachs
DESIGN FIRM
  Frankfurt Balkind Partners
DESIGNER
  David Suh

CLIENT
  CD Force
DESIGN FIRM
  Insight Design Communications
DESIGNERS
  Tracy Holdeman, Sherrie Holdeman

CLIENT
  Crossroads Communications
DESIGN FIRM
  Kellum McClain Inc.
DESIGNER
  Ron Kellum

CLIENT
  Drive Finanacial Services
DESIGN FIRM
  Kendall Creative Shop
DESIGNER
  Mark K. Platt

CLIENT
  St. Louis Blues
DESIGN FIRM
  Fleishman-Hillard Design, St. Louis
DESIGNER
  Buck Smith

# atmosphere

CLIENT
Atmoshpere Furniture, San Francisco
DESIGN FIRM
Fabian Geyrhalter
DESIGNER
Fabian Geyrhalter

# McKAY LANDING

CLIENT
Engle Homes/James Company
DESIGN FIRM
Noble Erickson Inc.
DESIGNERS
Steven Erickson, Robin Ridley

CLIENT
CallSmart
DESIGN FIRM
Insight Design Communications
DESIGNERS
Tracy Holdeman, Sherrie Holdeman

CLIENT
Kraft Innovative Applications
DESIGN FIRM
Brierton Design
DESIGNERS
Michael Brierton, Kirk Hitschel

CLIENT
AIA Maine - A Chapter of
The American Institute
of Architects
DESIGN FIRM
Jasper & Bridge
DESIGNER
Kim Noyes

CLIENT
OLA, LLC
DESIGN FIRM
Meteor Marketing
DESIGNER
Max Maxwell

HomeBuyer
Showroom.com℠
Builders & Home Buyers Selections Online

# WhyRunOut.com™

# PINCKNEY
## PHOTOGRAPHY

DISPLAYS • ADVERTISING

HORIZON

# SPRING CREEK
## Towers

miro

# FOX MEADOW

CLIENT
Engle Homes/James Company
DESIGN FIRM
Noble Erickson Inc.
DESIGNERS
Jackie Noble, Sarah Gandrud

# DATA DIMENSIONS

CLIENT
Data Dimensions
DESIGN FIRM
Walsh & Associates, Inc.
DESIGNER
Miriam Lisco

# DEPENDABLE
## DENTAL PLACEMENT

CLIENT
Dependable Dental Placement
DESIGN FIRM
Fred Pesce Design
DESIGNER
Fred Pesce

# *ExchangeSoft*

CLIENT
Exchange Soft
DESIGN FIRM
Austin William & Best
DESIGNER
Ron Dylnicki

CLIENT
San Luis Obispo Railroad Historical So.
DESIGN FIRM
Pierre Rademaker Design
DESIGNERS
Pierre Rademaker, Kenny B. Chávez

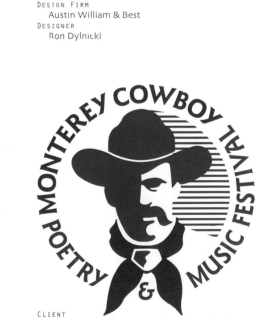

CLIENT
Monterey Cowboy Poetry & Music Festival
DESIGN FIRM
The Wecker Group
DESIGNER
Robert Wecker

## Scholarship Program

CLIENT
University of Illinois Foundation
DESIGN FIRM
Stan Gellman Graphic Design, Inc.
DESIGNERS
Barry Tilson, Erin Goter

# BRANDABLE
online.com

DESIGN FIRM
Zyrex, Inc.
DESIGNER
Erika Kao

**Digital Blackboard** *foundation*

CLIENT
Digital Blackboard Foundation
DESIGN FIRM
Walsh & Associates, Inc.
DESIGNERS
Miriam Lisco, Joann Kerr

CLIENT
La Strada Housing Development
DESIGN FIRM
Greenhaus
DESIGNERS
Tracy Sabin, Craig Fuller

SPIRIT OF THE CITY:

IMAGINING THE
PAN-AMERICAN
EXPOSITION

CLIENT
Buffalo and Erie County Historical Society
DESIGN FIRM
Crowley Webb & Associates
DESIGNER
Dave Buck

*the*edsite.com

CLIENT
Eovision
DESIGN FIRM
LPG Design
DESIGNERS
Lorna West, Chris West

CLIENT
San Francisco Ballet
DESIGN FIRM
Frankfurt Balkind Partners
DESIGNER
David Suh

CLIENT
De Jones Architexture
DESIGN FIRM
Insight Design Communications
DESIGNERS
Tracy Holdeman, Sherrie Holdeman

CLIENT
Beverly Jean Farris
DESIGN FIRM
The Marketing Store
DESIGNER
Calvina Yang Nguyen

CLIENT
The Climate Institute
DESIGN FIRM
Dever Designs
DESIGNER
Jeffrey L. Dever

CLIENT
Orange County
Performing Arts Center
DESIGN FIRM
Hayden Design
DESIGNERS
Tricia Hayden, Robert Hayden

CLIENT
St. Johns County V.C.B.
DESIGN FIRM
Gold & Associates
DESIGNER
Joe Varta

## BUFFALO PREP
*educating bright minority students*

CLIENT
Buffalo Prep
DESIGN FIRM
Crowley Webb & Associates
DESIGNER
Kelly Gambino

CLIENT
Warner Joest Builders
DESIGN FIRM
The Wecker Group
DESIGNERS
Robert Wecker, Tremayne Cryer

## ARBITRON

CLIENT
Arbitron
DESIGN FIRM
Smarteam Communications, Inc.
DESIGNERS
Gary Ridley, Brent Almond

## APTEGRA

CLIENT
Aptegra
DESIGN FIRM
Crowley Webb & Associates
DESIGNER
Ann Casady

## PILLSBURY WINTHROP LLP

CLIENT
Pillsbury Winthrop LLP
DESIGN FIRM
Greenfield/Belser Ltd.
DESIGNERS
Burkey Belser, Tony Marques

## Omnexus™  Informix®

CLIENT
Omnexus
DESIGN FIRM
Crowley Webb & Associates
DESIGNER
Brian Grunert

CLIENT
Informix
DESIGN FIRM
Frankfurt Balkind Partners
DESIGNER
David Suh

**CLIENT**
CMP
**DESIGN FIRM**
Frankfurt Balkind Partners
**DESIGNERS**
David Suh, Steven Fabrizio

**CLIENT**
Xactix
**DESIGN FIRM**
A to Z Corporate Logo
**DESIGNER**
Chris Konopack

**CLIENT**
Emarket Concepts
**DESIGN FIRM**
Mona MacDonald Design
**DESIGNER**
Mona MacDonald

**CLIENT**
annSwers
**DESIGN FIRM**
Aufuldish & Warinner
**DESIGNERS**
Bob Aufuldish, Kathy Warinner

OLSEN GRAFIX GROUP INC

**CLIENT**
Olsen Grafix Group, Inc.
**DESIGN FIRM**
Olsen Grafix Group, Inc.
**DESIGNER**
Dagfinn Olsen

**CLIENT**
Ketchum for Intersil
**DESIGN FIRM**
A to Z communications, inc.
**DESIGNER**
Aimee Lazer

The Aegis Group, Ltd

**CLIENT**
The Aegis Group, Ltd
**DESIGN FIRM**
Graves Fowler Associates
**DESIGNER**
Kristin Braaten

RECORDING • CREATIVE

**CLIENT**
Rainmaker Recording Creative
**DESIGN FIRM**
Hall & Partners

## CAESARS WORLD
# Baccarat
## *Invitational*

CLIENT
   Caesars Palace
DESIGN FIRM
   Creative Dynamics, Inc.
DESIGNERS
   Victor Rodriguez, Christopher Smith

CLIENT
   The Invisible Chef, Inc.
DESIGN FIRM
   Lia DiStefano
DESIGNER
   Lia DiStefano

CLIENT
   New Couple
DESIGN FIRM
   Aufuldish & Warinner
DESIGNER
   Kathy Warinner

CLIENT
   Purdue International Center
   For Entertainment Technology
DESIGN FIRM
   Purdue University
DESIGNER
   Li Zhang

CLIENT
   PocketDBA
DESIGN FIRM
   Liska + Associates, Inc.
DESIGNER
   Steve Liska

CLIENT
   Vertex
DESIGN FIRM
   Giraffe Design, Inc.
DESIGNER
   Jeffrey Bauer

CLIENT
   Greens.com
DESIGN FIRM
   The Golf Agency
DESIGNERS
   Tracy Sabin, Dann Wilson

# Thoroughbred
## Technologies

CLIENT
Thoroughbred Technologies
DESIGN FIRM
VIVIDESIGN Group
DESIGNERS
VIVIDESIGNGroup Staff

# KO'OLAU
## GOLF CLUB

CLIENT
Ko'olau Golf Club
DESIGN FIRM
Synergy Design
DESIGNER
Alan Low

CLIENT
Rutgers University - CEPA
DESIGN FIRM
Ananlysis/DoTart
DESIGNERS
Christine Lit, John Van Cleaf

CLIENT
Quickpen
DESIGN FIRM
Dietz Design Company
DESIGNER
Robert Zietz

# BANC
## SERVICES

CLIENT
Banc Services Group Inc.
DESIGN FIRM
Stan Gellman Graphic Design Inc.
DESIGNERS
Jill Lampen, Barry Tilson

CLIENT
Palace Casino Resort
DESIGN FIRM
The Prime TIme Group
DESIGNERS
Ted Riemann, John Seymour

CLIENT
Avanade
DESIGN FIRM
Landor Associates
DESIGNERS
Margaret Youngblood, Gail Taras,
Alessio Krauss

**avanade**<sup>SM</sup>

/systems.solutions.success/from Andersen Consulting & Microsoft

CLIENT
Beaumonde Day Spa
DESIGN FIRM
LPG Design
DESIGNER
Lorna West

SM

CLIENT
NCRIC Group, Inc.
DESIGN FIRM
Beveridge Seay Inc.
DESIGNERS
Nick Seay, David Feinstein,
Hubie Le

CLIENT
Visions Lighting
DESIGN FIRM
Hearken Creative Services
DESIGNER
Loren A. Roberts

CLIENT
Expresso Web
DESIGN FIRM
Never Boring Design Associates
DESIGNER
Lani Zuidervant

CLIENT
Featherstone Resort
DESIGN FIRM
Mühlhäuser & Young
DESIGNER
Barbara Mühlhäuser

CLIENT
Panda Management
DESIGN FIRM
Mike Salisbury, LLC
DESIGNERS
Mike Salisbury, Jill Bell,
Brian Sisson, Travis Page

**Dancing With The Mouse**

CLIENT
St. Johns County V.C.B.
DESIGN FIRM
Gold & Associates
DESIGNER
Keith Gold

CLIENT
National Dance Association – Kietha Manning
DESIGN FIRM
Wet Paper Bag Graphic Design
DESIGNER
Lewis Glaser

CLIENT
Manny's Underground
DESIGN FIRM
Noble Erickson Inc.
DESIGNERS
Steven Erickson, Sarah Gandrud

CLIENT
Dayton's
DESIGN FIRM
Shea
DESIGNER
Holly Utech

CLIENT
Ballena Vista Farm
DESIGN FIRM
Laura Coe Design Assoc.
DESIGNER
Ryoichi Yotsumoto

**NORTHWEST MUSEUM OF ARTS & CULTURE**

CLIENT
Lee & Hayes, PLLC
DESIGN FIRM
Klundt Hosmer Design
DESIGNERS
Lorri Feenan,
Darin Klundt

CLIENT
Ooh...Aaah!
DESIGN FIRM
Shea
DESIGNER
Pam McFerrin

CLIENT
Southeast Cardiovascular Group
DESIGN FIRM
Creative Communications & Graphics
DESIGNER
Greg Kunce

**RU•tv**
N E T W O R K ™

CLIENT
Rutgers University
DESIGN FIRM
Office of Print & Electronic Communications
DESIGNER
Joanne Dus-Zastrow

CLIENT
Del Webb Corporation
DESIGN FIRM
Estudio Ray
DESIGNERS
Joe Ray, Chris Ray, Leslie Link

**DDD**

CLIENT
DDD
DESIGN FIRM
Hamagami/Carroll & Assoc.
DESIGNER
Doris Kao

Saarman Construction

CLIENT
Saarman Construction
DESIGN FIRM
Bruce Yelaska Design
DESIGNER
Bruce Yelaska

# Hive4.com

CLIENT
Hive 4
DESIGN FIRM
Frankfurt Balkind Partners
DESIGNER
David Suh

## ULLICO
## Life Insurance
## Company

CLIENT
Ullico Life Insurance Company
DESIGN FIRM
Beveridge Seay, Inc.
DESIGNERS
Nick Seay, Hubie Le

CLIENT
Prometheus Publications –
Warren Klofkorn
DESIGN FIRM
Wet Paper Bag Graphic Design
DESIGNER
Lewis Glaser

CLIENT
Concept Interactive, Inc.
DESIGN FIRM
Kircher, Inc.
DESIGNER
Bruce E. Morgan

## Pots, Shears & Things

CLIENT
Bob Moore
DESIGN FIRM
Pensaré Design Group
DESIGNER
Kundia D. Wood

## News-Type Service, Inc.

CLIENT
News Type Service
DESIGN FIRM
Vince Rini Design
DESIGNER
Vince Rini

CLIENT
  Sea Ridge Housing Development
DESIGN FIRM
  Greenhaus
DESIGNERS
  Tracy Sabin, Craig Fuller,
  Sandra Sharp

CLIENT
  Matrix Solutions
DESIGN FIRM
  Kolano Design
DESIGNER
  Cate Sides

CLIENT
  ReturnView
DESIGN FIRM
  Laura Coe Design Assoc.
DESIGNERS
  Tracy Castle,
  Laura Coe Wright

CLIENT
  KSI Corporation
DESIGN FIRM
  Emphasis Seven Communications, Inc.
DESIGNER
  Craig Niedermaier

CLIENT
  Sabingrafik, Inc.
DESIGN FIRM
  Sabingrafik, Inc.
DESIGNER
  Tracy Sabin

CLIENT
  NK
DESIGN FIRM
  KUO Design
DESIGNER
  Bongchan Kim

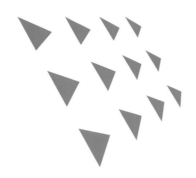

# Datacard™

## WORLDWIDE

CLIENT
Datacard
DESIGN FIRM
Frankfurt Balkind Partners
DESIGNER
David Suh

# Storage**Way**

CLIENT
StorageWay
DESIGN FIRM
Bruce Yelaska Design
DESIGNER
Bruce Yelaska

CLIENT
Mr. Recipe
DESIGN FIRM
De Santis Graphic Communications
DESIGNERS
Vanessa De Santis, Colleen Kennedy

CLIENT
Beers & Cutler
DESIGN FIRM
Grasp Creative, Inc.
DESIGNERS
Doug Fuller, Aaron Taylor,
Blake Stenning

# LEARNWRIGHT *llc*

CLIENT
Learnwright
DESIGN FIRM
Grasp Creative, Inc.
DESIGNER
Doug Fuller

# BOTANIC GARDEN
## OF WESTERN PENNSYLVANIA

CLIENT
The Horticultural Society of
Western Pennsylvania
DESIGN FIRM
Kolano Design
DESIGNER
Cate Sides

**RadioCentral**

CLIENT
  Radio Central
DESIGN FIRM
  Frankfurt Balkind Partners
DESIGNER
  David Suh

ETIENNE AIGNER

CLIENT
  Etienne Aigner
DESIGN FIRM
  Tangram Design Group, Inc.
DESIGNERS
  Tim Belair, Liu ping Leung

CHINATOWN
restaurant

CLIENT
  Chinatown Restaurant
DESIGN FIRM
  Power/Warner Communications Group, Inc.
DESIGNER
  Josie Fertig

CRAFTED CRYSTAL

CLIENT
  Princess House
DESIGN FIRM
  Kolano Design
DESIGNER
  Cate Sides

CLIENT
  Product Pop
DESIGN FIRM
  Anvil Graphic Design
DESIGNERS
  Cathy Chin, Laura Bauer

CLIENT
  Mambo
DESIGN FIRM
  Anvil Graphic Design, Inc.
DESIGNERS
  Gary Wong, Laura Bauer

CLIENT
Fast Iron Inc.
DESIGN FIRM
Studio Prima
DESIGNERS
Robert Perlman, Chris Harrington

CLIENT
Printing Industries Assoc.
of San Diego
DESIGN FIRM
Laura Coe Design Assoc.
DESIGNERS
Tom Richman,
Laura Coe Wright

CLIENT
The Wine Adviser
DESIGN FIRM
De Santis Graphic Communications
DESIGNER
Vanessa De Santis

CLIENT
Is It Art?
DESIGN FIRM
Robert Meyers Design
DESIGNER
Robert Meyers

CLIENT
Zeppelin Development
DESIGN FIRM
Noble Erickson Inc.
DESIGNERS
Steven Erickson, Noah Dempewolf

CLIENT
San Diego Zoo
DESIGN FIRM
Greenhaus
DESIGNERS
Tracy Sabin, Craig Fuller

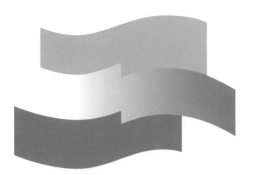

**Kybernin® P**

CLIENT
Advanstar Communications
DESIGN FIRM
O Design
DESIGNERS
Bong Chan Kim, Claire Bonahoom

CLIENT
M2 Communications/Aventis
DESIGN FIRM
O Design
DESIGNER
Claire Bonahoom

EASTSIDE

**SUNSHINE** preschool

CLIENT
The Mosites Company
DESIGN FIRM
Kolano Design
DESIGNER
Cate Sides

CLIENT
Sunshine Preschool
DESIGN FIRM
Willoughby Design
DESIGNER
Garrett Burke

CLIENT
Archway-Mother's Cookies
DESIGN FIRM
Axion Design Inc.

CLIENT
Celio Groves
DESIGN FIRM
Axion Design Inc.

INTERCONNECT SERVICES, INC.

CLIENT
Interconnect Services Inc.
DESIGN FIRM
RG Design
DESIGNER
Russ Garn

CLIENT
Old Mutual Properties
DESIGN FIRM
Development Design Group
DESIGNER
Kevin Kern

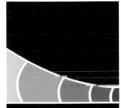 SUBMEDIA

CLIENT
Submedia, LLC
DESIGN FIRM
O Design
DESIGNER
Jason B. Cohen

CLIENT
Mountain Dell Grill
DESIGN FIRM
Lara Mullen
DESIGNER
Lara Mullen

CLIENT
Dairy.com
DESIGN FIRM
Edelman Public Relations
DESIGNERS
Marilyn Dawson, Joe Ondrla,
Mary Huffman

KINZAN

CLIENT
Kinzan
DESIGN FIRM
Visual Asylum
DESIGNER
Joel Sotelo

CLIENT
Just Add Guests
DESIGN FIRM
Foley Sackett, Inc.
DESIGNER
Michelle Willinganz

CLIENT
Village Coffee Co.
DESIGN FIRM
Graif Design
DESIGNER
Matt Graif

e v o **|** v e

CLIENT
Evolve Developments, LLC.
DESIGN FIRM
Pensaré Design Group
DESIGNER
Kundia D. Wood

c****nnection™
CARDS

CLIENT
Aventis
DESIGN FIRM
Pensaré Design Group
DESIGNER
Kundia D. Wood

water·color℠
*A Southern Coastal Landscape.* **FLORIDA**

CLIENT
Arvida
DESIGN FIRM
David Carter Design Associates
DESIGNERS
Sharon LeJeune, Paul Munsterman

OUTLOOK HEIGHTS

CLIENT
Dividend Homes
DESIGN FIRM
Gauger & Silva
DESIGNERS
Bob Ankers, Aurielle Getas

# P E A R L   M O O N
## B O U T I Q U E

**Client**
Mandalay Bay Resort & Casino
**Design Firm**
David Carter Design Associates
**Designer**
Tabitha Bogard

## DUBLIN RANCH

**Client**
Dublin Ranch
**Design Firm**
Gauger & Silva
**Designer**
Lori Murphy

**Client**
HCIA Sachs
**Design Firm**
McKnight Kurland Baccelli

**Client**
WebPartner
**Design Firm**
Vislgy
**Designers**
Suzy Leung, Linda Kelley

**Client**
Mindstep
**Design Firm**
Paradowski Graphic Design
**Designer**
Steve Cox

**Client**
Student Buy.com
**Design Firm**
Mastandrea Design, Inc.
**Designer**
Mary Anne Mastandrea

CLIENT
Coop's Skycap Service
DESIGN FIRM
Deutsch Design Works
DESIGNERS
Barry Deutsch, Jess Giambroni

CLIENT
Peet's Coffee & Tea
DESIGN FIRM
Enterprise/IG
DESIGNER
Phillip Ting

CLIENT
Avicon
DESIGN FIRM
Doerr Associates
DESIGNER
Lauren Jevick

CLIENT
JustGive.org
DESIGN FIRM
Diesel Design
DESIGNERS
Amy Bainbridge, Luiz Dominguez

CLIENT
ePeople
DESIGN FIRM
1185 Design
DESIGNERS
Peggy Burke, Rachael Parakh

CLIENT
Ajunto
DESIGN FIRM
D4 Creative Group
DESIGNER
Wicky Wai-Kuen Lee

richard
PELLICCI

CLIENT
Richard Pellicci
DESIGN FIRM
Pensaré Design Group
DESIGNER
Yihong Hsu

Consultant
Dietitians
in Health Care Facilities

CLIENT
Consultant Dietitians
DESIGN FIRM
Minx Design
DESIGNER
Cecilia Sveda

APTIMUS

CLIENT
Aptimus
DESIGN FIRM
Hornall Anderson Design Works
DESIGNERS
Katha Dalton, Bruce Branson-Meyer,
Michael Brugman, Tobi Brown,
Mary Hermes, Ed Lee, Taka Suzuki

Hungry Minds™

CLIENT
Hungry Minds
DESIGN FIRM
Addis
DESIGNERS
Kristine Hung, Ron Vandenberg, Chris Nagle

CALIBRE

CLIENT
First Union
DESIGN FIRM
Gibson Creative
DESIGNERS
Kelly Bush, Dina Lyons,
Juliette Brown

cobion

CLIENT
Cobion
DESIGN FIRM
Visigy
DESIGNERS
Chelsea Hernandez, Ken Skistimas

CLIENT
iAsiaWorks, Inc.
DESIGN FIRM
Gee + Chung Design
DESIGNERS
Earl Gee, Kay Wu

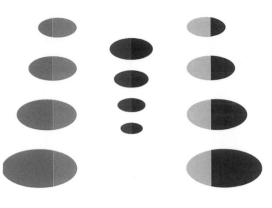

## Metropolitan Hotel

CLIENT
Metropolitan Hotel
DESIGN FIRM
Ziccardi & Partners
DESIGNERS
Tracy Brennan, Nassos Gnafkis

CLIENT
Papermoon Studios
DESIGN FIRM
Agnew Moyer Smith Inc.
DESIGNERS
John Sotirakis, Kurt Hess, Jack Kelley

CLIENT
CPS Communications
DESIGN FIRM
Tom Fowler, Inc.
DESIGNER
Thomas G. Fowler

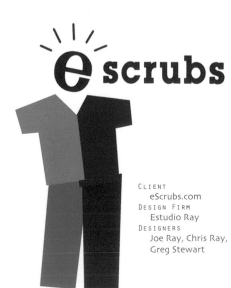

CLIENT
eScrubs.com
DESIGN FIRM
Estudio Ray
DESIGNERS
Joe Ray, Chris Ray,
Greg Stewart

CLIENT
The Fitness Choice
DESIGN FIRM
[i]e design
DESIGNER
Marcie Carson

The
Fitness Choice

# W O R D W A V E ᔆᴹ

CLIENT
Word Wave
DESIGN FIRM
Partners + Simons
DESIGNER
Lisa Stevenson

## Halloween
## Spooktakular

CLIENT
Akron Symphony Orchestra
DESIGN FIRM
Minx Design
DESIGNER
Cecilia Sveda

CLIENT
MAS Global Enterprises
DESIGN FIRM
Stein & Company
DESIGNERS
Stein Creative Team

CLIENT
Cross Creek Golf Club
DESIGN FIRM
Rieches Baird
DESIGNERS
Holly Mueller, Anant Panchal

CLIENT
Marriott International
DESIGN FIRM
WorkHorse Creative
DESIGNER
David Vogin

CLIENT
Water's Edge Gardening
DESIGN FIRM
Shields Design
DESIGNER
Charles Shields

**CLIENT**
Price Contracting, Inc.
**DESIGN FIRM**
Empire Communications Group
**DESIGNER**
Phil Helow

**CLIENT**
NIAF (National Italian American Foundation)
**DESIGN FIRM**
Supon Design Group
**DESIGNERS**
Supon Phornirunlit, Brent Almond,
Pum Mek-Aroonreung

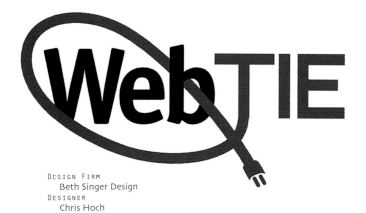

**DESIGN FIRM**
Beth Singer Design
**DESIGNER**
Chris Hoch

**the currency of speed**

**CLIENT**
Omni Pin
**DESIGN FIRM**
McKnight Kurland Baccelli

**CLIENT**
Sonoma County Tourism Program
**DESIGN FIRM**
Muhlhauser & Young
**DESIGNER**
Barbara Muhlhauser

**CLIENT**
Spectrum Field Services
**DESIGN FIRM**
Striegel and Associates
**DESIGNERS**
Brandon Taylor, Belinda Hedgecock

# Quantapoint™

**CLIENT**
Quantapoint
**DESIGN FIRM**
Agnew Moyer Smith Inc.
**DESIGNERS**
Lisa Vitalbo, Randy Ziegler,
Geoge Heidekat

# WEB 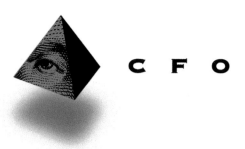 CFO

**CLIENT**
Web CFO
**DESIGN FIRM**
Twist
**DESIGNER**
Chris Rossi

# invirion

**CLIENT**
Bruce Patterson/Invirion
**DESIGN FIRM**
Crosby Associates Inc.
**DESIGNERS**
Malgorzata Sobus, Bart Crosby

# ˆimpli

**CLIENT**
Impli
**DESIGN FIRM**
Hornall Anderson Design Works
**DESIGNERS**
Jack Anderson, Sonja Max,
Kathy Saito, Alan Copeland

# CONVERA™

**CLIENT**
Convera
**DESIGN FIRM**
Michael Patrick Partners
**DESIGNERS**
Dan O'Brien, Connie Hwang,
Eko Tjoek, Brian Hilton

# outride™

**CLIENT**
Outride
**DESIGN FIRM**
Michael Patrick Partners
**DESIGNERS**
Devin Muldoon, Connie Hwang,
Matt Rowland, Jeong Kim

# TALENT ARCHITECTS

CLIENT
Talent Architects
DESIGN FIRM
DAM Creative Incorporated
DESIGNER
Dana A. Meek

# AWOLPET.COM

CLIENT
Astrachan Communications
DESIGN FIRM
McMillian Design
DESIGNERS
William McMillian, Mike Astrachan

THE MISS AMERICA ORGANIZATION

CLIENT
Miss America Organization
DESIGN FIRM
Sullivan Marketing
& Communications
DESIGNER
Jack Sullivan

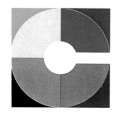

# COLOR FX

CLIENT
ColorFX - Printing Company
DESIGN FIRM
Mauck & Associates
DESIGNERS
Scott Thornton, Kent Mauck

tantivy

CLIENT
Tantivy
DESIGN FIRM
Edelman Public Relations
DESIGNERS
John Avila, Josh Witherspoon

# POWERTIE™

CLIENT
G-Commerce
DESIGN FIRM
Handler Design Group, Inc.
DESIGNER
Bruce Handler

Z E N E R G Y

CLIENT
Zenergy
DESIGN FIRM
Visigy
DESIGNERS
Chelsea Hernandez, Chris Ardito

CLIENT
Charlotte Country Day School
DESIGN FIRM
Set?Communicate!
DESIGNER
Steve Thomas

Neothermia

CLIENT
Neothermia
DESIGN FIRM
Artemis Creative, Inc.
DESIGNERS
Wes Aoki, Gary Nusinow

health science
COMMUNICATIONS

CLIENT
Health Science Communications, Inc.
DESIGN FIRM
Health Science Communications, Inc.
DESIGNER
Robert Padovano

FOREST
MEADOWS
A Richland Community

CLIENT
Richland Development Corp.
DESIGN FIRM
Epstein Design Partners
DESIGNER
Marla Gutzwiller

Katten Muchin Zavis

K          M          Z

CLIENT
Katten Muchin Zavis
DESIGN FIRM
Crosby Associates Inc.
DESIGNERS
Bart Crosby, Malgorzato Sobus

# CASTILE VENTURES

CLIENT
Castile Ventures
DESIGN FIRM
Gee + Chung Design
DESIGNER
Earl Gee

# gigabeat™

CLIENT
Gigabeat
DESIGN FIRM
1185 Design
DESIGNERS
Peggy Burke, Veta Brandel

# Netigy℠

CLIENT
Netigy Corporation
DESIGN FIRM
Gee + Chung Design
DESIGNERS
Earl Gee, Kay Wu

**AerialWAVE**
*Cellular and PCS Testing*

CLIENT
Aerial Wave
DESIGN FIRM
Spark Design
DESIGNER
Joe Gunsten

# BUILT2XL

CLIENT
Built2XL
DESIGN FIRM
Supon Design Group
DESIGNERS
Supon Phornirunlit,
Todd Metrokin

# geron

CLIENT
Geron
DESIGN FIRM
Howry Design Associates
DESIGNERS
Jill Howry, Clay Williams

# PaperSource

CLIENT
Paper Source Hawaii
DESIGN FIRM
Synergy Design
DESIGNER
Alan Low

# Offset Atlanta

CLIENT
Offset Atlanta
DESIGN FIRM
Worldstar Design
DESIGNER
Greg Guhl

CLIENT
Cabana Restaurant & Bar
DESIGN FIRM
Graif Design
DESIGNER
Matt Graif

CLIENT
Eviciti Corporation
DESIGN FIRM
Crosby Associates Inc.
DESIGNER
Bart Crosby

# EMPLOYMENT LINK

CLIENT
Envision Boulder
DESIGN FIRM
Pollman Marketing Arts, Inc.
DESIGNER
Jennifer Pollman

# OMNIPIN

CLIENT
Omni Pin
DESIGN FIRM
McKnight Kurland Baccelli

CLIENT
G. Lazzara
DESIGN FIRM
Icon Graphics, Inc.
DESIGNERS
Icon Graphics, Inc.

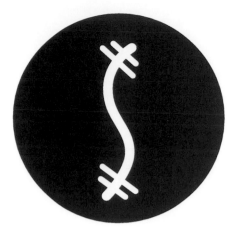

CLIENT
Beth Steinke - Personal Training
DESIGN FIRM
McMillian Design
DESIGNER
William McMillian

CLIENT
Courier One
DESIGN FIRM
Watt/Fleishman-Hillard
DESIGNER
Margaret Ess

CLIENT
Professional Internship Program
DESIGN FIRM
Fred Pesce Design
DESIGNER
Fred Pesce

CLIENT
Brand Harvest
DESIGN FIRM
Supon Design Group
DESIGNERS
Supon Phornirunlit, Tom Klinedinst

CLIENT
Main Line Oncology Hematology Associates
DESIGN FIRM
Bailey Design Group
DESIGNERS
Wendy Slavish, Jerry Corcoran

# MUKHAMBAZI
wine bar

CLIENT
Marriott International
DESIGN FIRM
WorkHorse Creative
DESIGNERS
David Vogin, Lesley Quesada

**H&R BLOCK**®

CLIENT
H & R Block
DESIGN FIRM
Landor Associates
DESIGNERS
Margaret Youngblood, Cameron Imani,
Eric Scott, Kisitina Wong, Tina Schoepflin,
Irena Blok, David Rockwell, Mary Hayano

CLIENT
Art Center College
of Design Alumni Council
DESIGN FIRM
Gee + Chung Design
DESIGNER
Earl Gee

CLIENT
Network Associates
DESIGN FIRM
1185 Design
DESIGNERS
Peggy Burke, Veta Brandel,
Joan Takenaka

CLIENT
The Women's Community Clinic
DESIGN FIRM
Pandora
DESIGNER
Silvia Grossmann

CLIENT
Alter Ego Networks
DESIGN FIRM
1185 Design
DESIGNERS
Peggy Burke, Jason Chan, John Milly

CLIENT
E*TRADE
DESIGN FIRM
Michael Patrick Partners
DESIGNERS
Dan O'Brien, Matt Sanders,
Connie Hwang

**BrainShare2000**

CLIENT
Novell, Inc.
DESIGN FIRM
Hornall Anderson Design Works
DESIGNERS
Larry Anderson, Jack Anderson,
James Tee, Holly Craven,
Michael Brugman, Kaye Farmer

CLIENT
Dechert
DESIGN FIRM
Bailey Design Group
DESIGNERS
Dave Fiedler, Gary LaCroix

CLIENT
University of Chicago
Graduate School of Business
DESIGN FIRM
Crosby Associates Inc.
DESIGNER
Bart Crosby

CLIENT
Covigo
DESIGN FIRM
Michael Patrick Partners
DESIGNERS
Mike Mescall, Connie Hwang,
Ian Smith, Sam Chew

CLIENT
Flowery Beauty Products
DESIGN FIRM
Cullinane Design
DESIGNER
Carmen Li

**PRISM**
Color Corporation

CLIENT
Prism Color Corporation
DESIGN FIRM
D4 Creative Group
DESIGNER
Wicky Wai-Kuen Lee

project grace

CLIENT
Project Grace
DESIGN FIRM
FLUID
DESIGNERS
Blake DeJonge, Tom Crimp

**ADOBE CREEK**

CLIENT
Adobe Creek
DESIGN FIRM
Halleck
DESIGNER
Arlene Horwitz

**peoplepc**

CLIENT
People PC
DESIGN FIRM
Landor Associates
DESIGNERS
Margaret Youngblood, Patrick Cox,
Fred Averin, Gaston Yagmourian

**SONIC blue**™

CLIENT
SONICblue
DESIGN FIRM
Addison Whitney
DESIGNER
David Houk

**TRUETIME**

CLIENT
TrueTime
DESIGN FIRM
Visigy
DESIGNERS
Suzy Leung, Linda Kelley

peoplebusinessnetwork™

People working better.

CLIENT
People Business Network
DESIGN FIRM
C&A
DESIGNER
Ken Thorlton

MeetingMakers.com

CLIENT
MeetingMakers.com
DESIGN FIRM
2 Mind Design
DESIGNER
Dave Gilman

THE ADVANCED | Travel Group

CLIENT
Advanced Travel
DESIGN FIRM
Sargent & Berman
DESIGNER
Taleen Bedikian

QUELLOS
GROUP, LLC

CLIENT
Quellos Group
DESIGN FIRM
Belyea
DESIGNER
Ron Lars Hansen

UNITED
WIRELESS

the warhol:

CLIENT
United Wireless
DESIGN FIRM
Design Room
DESIGNER
Chad Gordon

CLIENT
The Andy Warhol Museum
DESIGN FIRM
Agnew Moyer Smith Inc.
DESIGNERS
John Sotirakis, Lisa Vitalbo, Gina Datres

**GRASP**

CLIENT
   Grasp Creative, Inc.
DESIGN FIRM
   Grasp Creative, Inc.
DESIGNERS
   Doug Fuller, Aaron Taylor

**Eyeball.com**™

CLIENT
   Eyeball.com
DESIGN FIRM
   Diesel Design
DESIGNER
   Amy Bainbridge

**STRUXICON**™

CLIENT
   Struxicon.com
DESIGN FIRM
   Hershey Associates
DESIGNER
   Lisa Joss

**Camp Jenney**

*The Camp For Kids With Cystic Fibrosis*

CLIENT
   American Lung Association
DESIGN FIRM
   Dotzler Creative Arts

**mobshop**

CLIENT
   Mobshop
DESIGN FIRM
   Diesel Design
DESIGNERS
   Aaron Morton, Emily Cohen

**AUSTIN, WILLIAMS & BEST**

ADVERTISING AND MARKETING

CLIENT
   Austin Williams & Best
DESIGN FIRM
   Austin Williams & Best
DESIGNERS
   Fred Pesce

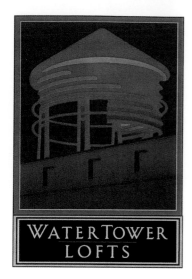

PRODUCERS &
ENGINEERS WING

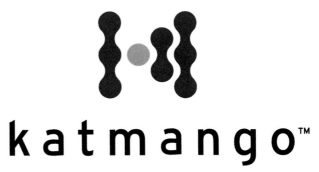

eClipse

katmango™

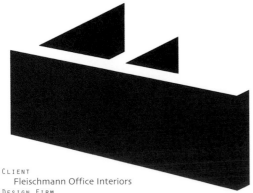

**For U.S. Senate**
# Hillary

CLIENT
Hillary for US Senate
DESIGN FIRM
Taylor Design & DeVito/Verdi Advertising
DESIGNERS
Daniel Taylor, Hannah Fichandler,
Mike Samuel

c o w ● p a r a d e™

CLIENT
Cow Parade Worldwide LLC
DESIGN FIRM
Supon Design Group
DESIGNERS
Supon Phornirunlit, Brent Almond,
Jae Wee

**heritage graphics**
**inc.**

CLIENT
Heritage Graphics Inc.
DESIGN FIRM
Estudio Ray
DESIGNERS
Joe Ray, Chris Ray,
Greg Stewart

go4service.com

CLIENT
Go For Service
DESIGN FIRM
Inc 3
DESIGNERS
Harvey Appelbaum, Micah Monserat

# TEXERE

CLIENT
Texere
DESIGN FIRM
Mastandrea Design, Inc.
DESIGNER
Mary Anne Mastandrea

# PRIMAVERA
*Italian Grill*

CLIENT
Marriott International
DESIGN FIRM
WorkHorse Creative
DESIGNERS
David Vogin, James Hersick

CLIENT
Detroit Rockers
DESIGN FIRM
FCS, Inc.
DESIGNERS
Frank Fisher, Jackie Green

CLIENT
NetLondon.com
DESIGN FIRM
Shields Design
DESIGNER
Charles Shields

CLIENT
Circle Group Inc.
DESIGN FIRM
Watt/Fleishman-Hillard
DESIGNER
Russ Hirth

CLIENT
The Kirlin Foundation
DESIGN FIRM
Methodologie, Inc.
DESIGNERS
Gabe Goldman, Christopher Downs

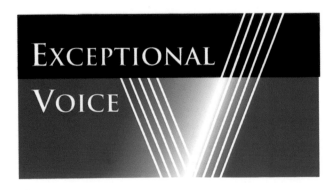

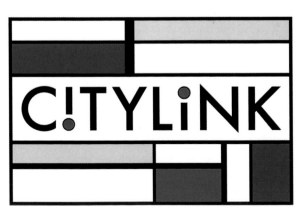

CLIENT
Exceptional Voice
DESIGN FIRM
Pollman Marketing Arts, Inc.
DESIGNERS
Jennifer Pollman, Leslie Blanton

CLIENT
HongKong Land (Esplanade) Ltd.
DESIGN FIRM
Calori & Vanden - Eynden
DESIGNERS
David Vanden-Eynden, Chris Calori, Judy Gee

## SCHWENKE

DESIGN & BUILD, INC

CLIENT
Schwenke Design & Build
DESIGN FIRM
Graif Design
DESIGNER
Matt Graif

CLIENT
Hasbro
DESIGN FIRM
Mike Salisbury, LLC
DESIGNERS
Mike Salisbury,
Dave Willardson, Bob Maile

CLIENT
Screenvision Cinema Promotions
DESIGN FIRM
INC 3
DESIGNER
Harvey Appelbaum, Ayse Celem

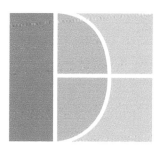

## DORSKY
## HODGSON
## +
## PARTNERS

CLIENT
Dorsky Hodgson & Partners, Inc.
DESIGN FIRM
Epstein Design Partners
DESIGNER
Marla Gutzwiller

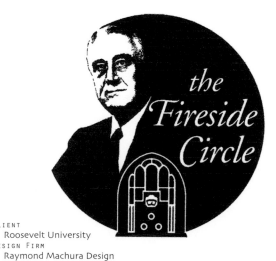

CLIENT
Roosevelt University
DESIGN FIRM
Raymond Machura Design
DESIGNER
Ramond Machura

CLIENT
Affinity Group
DESIGN FIRM
Mark Oliver, Inc.
DESIGNER
Mark Oliver

# bp

CLIENT
BP Amoco
DESIGN FIRM
Landor Associates
DESIGNERS
Margaret Youngblood, Nancy Hoefig, Courtney Reeser,
David Zapata, Brad Scott, Cynthia Murnane, Todd True,
Frank Mueller, Michele Berry, Ivan Thelin, Ladd Woodland,
Maria Wenzel

CLIENT
Interactive Expert Systems LLC
DESIGN FIRM
Watt/Fleishman-Hillard
DESIGNER
Kurt Roscoe

CLIENT
Worldwide Wings
DESIGN FIRM
Mike Salisbury, LLC
DESIGNER
Nina Weissbeck

# VoiceLink
## COMMUNICATIONS

CLIENT
VoiceLink Communications
DESIGN FIRM
Empire Communications Group
DESIGNER
Phil Helow

# ELM RIDGE Value Advisors, LLC

CLIENT
Elm Ridge
DESIGN FIRM
INC 3
DESIGNERS
Harvey Appelbaum, Ayse Celem

# ENTRANSIT
### Engine for the Information Movement

CLIENT
Entransit, Inc.
DESIGN FIRM
O&J Design, Inc.
DESIGNERS
Andrezej Olejniczak, Jun Lee

**CLIENT**
Montana Eyes
**DESIGN FIRM**
Mike Salisbury, LLC
**DESIGNERS**
Travis Page, Nina Weissbeck,
Mike Salisbury

**CLIENT**
TAG Toys, Inc.
**DESIGN FIRM**
Shimokochi/Reeves
**DESIGNERS**
Mamoru Shimokochi, Anne Reeves

**BULABAY**™

**CLIENT**
Bulabay
**DESIGN FIRM**
1185 Design
**DESIGNERS**
Peggy Burke, Peter Cassell, Julia Foug

**CLIENT**
Grace King
**DESIGN FIRM**
INC 3
**DESIGNERS**
Harvey Appelbaum, Nick Guarracino

**CLIENT**
Fitness Today, Corporation
**DESIGN FIRM**
Shimokochi/Reeves
**DESIGNERS**
Mamoru Shimokochi, Anne Reeves

**CLIENT**
DJJ Technologies
**DESIGN FIRM**
Handler Design Group, Inc.
**DESIGNER**
Bruce Handler

# Fulton Street Mall

DESIGN FIRM
Calori & Vanden - Eynden
DESIGNERS
Chris Calori, Denise Funaro

# Digeno
## AN RR DONNELLEY COMPANY

CLIENT
RR Donnelly & Sons
DESIGN FIRM
Landor Associates
DESIGNERS
Margaret Youngblood, Matteo Vianello

CLIENT
East3
DESIGN FIRM
Rodgers Townsend
DESIGNER
Luke Partridge

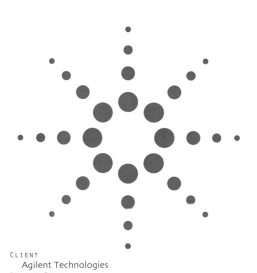

CLIENT
Agilent Technologies
DESIGN FIRM
Landor Associates
DESIGNERS
Erick Scott, Doug Sellers, Steve Holler, Joe Stitzlein,
Kisitina Wong, Kieth Trickett, Meritxell Grau

# Charlotte
## Bockhold Russell
### WATERCOLORS
*Proverbs 3:5 "Trust in the Lord with all of your heart..."*

CLIENT
Charlotte Bockhold Russell
DESIGN FIRM
Miller & White Advertising
DESIGNER
Jenny Hoffeditz

CLIENT
NCCAM (National Center
for Complementary & Alternative Medicine
DESIGN FIRM
HC Creative Communications
DESIGNER
Jessica Palombo

CLIENT
Advicezone.com
DESIGN FIRM
Supon Design Group
DESIGNERS
Supon Phornirunlit, Pum Mek-Aroonreung,
Michole Howley

CLIENT
Vulcan Northwest
DESIGN FIRM
Michael Courtney Design
DESIGNERS
Mike Courtney, Scott Souchock

CLIENT
Singer Direct
DESIGN FIRM
Inc3
DESIGNERS
Harvey Appelbaum, Micah Monserat

**BRIDGESPAN**™

Where Trust and Technology Connect™

CLIENT
BridgeSpan
DESIGN FIRM
Howry Design Associates
DESIGNERS
Jill Howry, Clay Williams

**portable** life ™

*Mobility starts here*

CLIENT
Portable Life.com
DESIGN FIRM
Howry Design Associates
DESIGNERS
Jill Howry, Clay Williams

VIANOVUS

CLIENT
Vianovus
DESIGN FIRM
Twist
DESIGNER
Lori Reed

CLIENT
Mike Salisbury
DESIGN FIRM
Mike Salisbury, LLC
DESIGNERS
Ziska Guenther, Mike Salisbury

CLIENT
Bungee Software
DESIGN FIRM
Mike Salisbury, LLC
DESIGNERS
Derek Harven, Tor Naerheim

CLIENT
Hallmark Custom Homes
DESIGN FIRM
Carolyn J. Hunter Advertising
DESIGNERS
Carolyn J. Hunter

CLIENT
American Workgear
DESIGN FIRM
Fred Pesce Design
DESIGNER
Fred Pesce

CLIENT
General Magic
DESIGN FIRM
Mortensen Design
DESIGNERS
PJ Niecker, Gordon Mortensen

CLIENT
Bass Litho
DESIGN FIRM
Graif Design
DESIGNER
Matt Rose

CLIENT
Food Marketing Institute
DESIGN FIRM
Kircher, Inc.
DESIGNER
Bruce E. Morgan

CLIENT
Allegheny County
Airport Authority
DESIGN FIRM
Sewickley Graphics & Design, Inc.
DESIGNER
Jim Reybein

# FRIENDS

## OF LOS GATOS PUBLIC LIBRARY

CLIENT
Friends of Los Gatos Public Library
DESIGN FIRM
Patt Mann Berry Design
DESIGNERS
Patt Mann Berry, Alice McKown

CLIENT
Metal Spectrum
DESIGN FIRM
Edelman Public Relations
DESIGNERS
Marilyn Dawson, Joe Ondrla

CLIENT
Rapido's
DESIGN FIRM
Design Forum
DESIGNERS
Bruce Dybrad, Vivenne Padillia

CLIENT
Doughmakers, LLC
DESIGN FIRM
Miller & White Advertising
DESIGNERS
Jenny Hoffeditz, Melissa Gausmann

**CLIENT**
The LTC Group
**DESIGN FIRM**
Liquid Graphix/The LTC Group

**CLIENT**
Merv Griffin
**DESIGN FIRM**
Mike Salisbury, LLC
**DESIGNERS**
Leslie Carbaga, Brian Sisson,
Jim Shoemaker

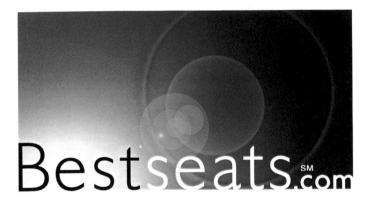

**CLIENT**
BestSeats
**DESIGN FIRM**
Addis
**DESIGNER**
Erica Kwei, Debbie Smith,
Ron Vandenberg

**CLIENT**
86.com
**DESIGN FIRM**
Gibson Creative
**DESIGNER**
Juliette Brown

**CLIENT**
Connect.me
**DESIGN FIRM**
Levin Breidenbach Wade
**DESIGNER**
Jeff Breidenbach

**CLIENT**
Vectis
**DESIGN FIRM**
Addis
**DESIGNERS**
Ron Vandenberg, Bob Hullinger,
Glen Spencer

**WHITEBOX advisors**

CLIENT
Whitebox Advisors
DESIGN FIRM
Tilka Design
DESIGNERS
Jane Tilka, Shannon Shriver

**ResQSoft**

CLIENT
ResQSoft
DESIGN FIRM
EVD Advertising
DESIGNER
Marc Foelsch

**CYMERC**
THE IT EXCHANGE

CLIENT
Cymerc Exchange
DESIGN FIRM
Extraprise Group, Inc.
DESIGNERS
Colin O'Neill, Amanda Swanson,
Julie Tsuchiya, Mark Sloneker

**MILLENNIA**

CLIENT
General Services Administration
DESIGN FIRM
Grasp Creative, Inc.
DESIGNER
Blake Stenning

**TWELVE HORSES**

CLIENT
Twelve Horses
DESIGN FIRM
Hornall Anderson Design Works
DESIGNERS
Jack Anderson, Lisa Cerveny,
Mary Chin Hutchison, Don Stayner

CLIENT
Charlotte Country Day School
DESIGN FIRM
Set?Communicate!
DESIGNER
Steve Thomas

Courtesy of LucasArts Entertainment Company LLC

CLIENT
LucasArts Entertainment Company
DESIGN FIRM
B.D. Fox & Friends
DESIGNER
Garrett Burke

CLIENT
Articulate Inc.
DESIGN FIRM
Robert Meyers Design
DESIGNER
Robert Meyers

Courtesy of LucasArts Entertainment Company LLC

CLIENT
LucasArts Entertainment Company
DESIGN FIRM
B.D. Fox & Friends
DESIGNER
Brett Wooldridge

CLIENT
Articulate Inc.
DESIGN FIRM
Robert Meyers Design
DESIGNER
Robert Meyers

Courtesy of LucasArts Entertainment Company LLC

CLIENT
LucasArts Entertainment Company
DESIGN FIRM
B.D. Fox & Friends
DESIGNERS
Mark Weinstein, Garrett Burke,
Chris Reardon

CLIENT
Articulate Inc.
DESIGN FIRM
Robert Meyers Design
DESIGNER
Robert Meyers

CLIENT
Children's Museum (CM2)
DESIGN FIRM
Grady Britton
DESIGNER
Jeni Stewart

CLIENT
Partners + Simons
DESIGN FIRM
Partners + Simons
DESIGNER
Lisa Stevenson

CLIENT
Sinotrans
DESIGN FIRM
Orient Communications
DESIGNERS
Doug Wadden, Alice Hung

CLIENT
Truck Bay
DESIGN FIRM
Hornall Anderson Design Works

digital solutions group

CLIENT
The LTC Group
DESIGN FIRM
The LTC Group/Liquid Graphix

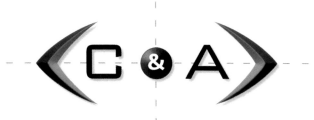

Clarke & Associates

CLIENT
C & A
DESIGN FIRM
C & A
DESIGNER
Heather Weimer

E M P Y R E A N

CLIENT
Empyrean Capital Group, LLC
DESIGN FIRM
WINDIGO
DESIGNERS
Lia Di Stefano,
James Gubelmann

COMMUNICATIONS
360

CLIENT
Linda Connor
DESIGN FIRM
Paradowski Graphic Design
DESIGNER
Alex Paradowski

Ryan Communications

CLIENT
Susan Ryan
DESIGN FIRM
Paradowski Graphic Design
DESIGNER
Alex Paradowski

du PARC

CLIENT
Paris Casino Resort
DESIGN FIRM
David Carter Design Associates
DESIGNER
Tabitha Bogard

DPG
DIGITAL PRODUCTION GROUP

CLIENT
Digital Production Group
DESIGN FIRM
Shields Design
DESIGNER
Tom Kimmelman

MONTEL

CLIENT
Paramount Pictures
DESIGN FIRM
Design Lab @ Broadway Video
DESIGNER
Gary Keenan

**CLIENT**
Trillicom-Data Architects
**DESIGN FIRM**
Shook
**DESIGNERS**
Dave Gibson, Ginger Riley

# ThemeMarks™

**CLIENT**
Fox River Papers
**DESIGN FIRM**
Design North, Inc.
**DESIGNER**
Mark Topczewski

**CLIENT**
Javelin
**DESIGN FIRM**
Hornall Anderson Design Works
**DESIGNERS**
Jack Anderson, James Tee, Henry Yiu

# cleanwave™

**YOUR ONLINE LAUNDRY SERVICE**

**CLIENT**
Cleanwave
**DESIGN FIRM**
Enterprise/IG
**DESIGNER**
Amy Hershman

**CLIENT**
iVantage Bank Corp.
**DESIGN FIRM**
Lipson Alport Glass & Assoc.
**DESIGNER**
Katherine Hoderied

# Lilly

**CLIENT**
Eil Lilly & Company
**DESIGN FIRM**
Landor Associates
**DESIGNERS**
Margaret Youngblood, Frank Mueller,
Michele Berry, Pia Carino, John Bowers,
Brad Scott, Rebecca Titcomb

Apenberry's
Cultivating the Garden Personality

Apenberry's
Cultivating the Garden Personality

Apenberry's
Cultivating the Garden Personality

**CLIENT**
Zolotrips
**DESIGN FIRM**
Diesel Design
**DESIGNERS**
Aaron Morton, Amy Bainbridge

**CLIENT**
Apenberry's
**DESIGN FIRM**
Magic Pencil Studios
**DESIGNERS**
Scott Feldman, Billy Davis

OVERTON
& ASSOCIATES

**CLIENT**
Overton & Associates
**DESIGN FIRM**
Grasp Creative, Inc.
**DESIGNERS**
Sarina Mokhtar, Minh Ta

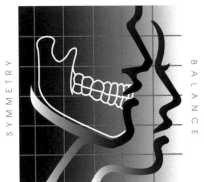

PROPORTION

SYMMETRY

BALANCE

ORAL & FACIAL
SURGERY CENTER

**CLIENT**
Oral & Facial Surgery Center
**DESIGN FIRM**
Sullivan Marketing & Communications
**DESIGNER**
Jack Sullivan

**CLIENT**
Bay Area Jewish Healing Center
**DESIGN FIRM**
Bobby Reich-Patri GRAFIX
**DESIGNER**
Bobby Reich-Patri

Bay Area
Jewish Healing
Center

**CLIENT**
Doug Lee
**DESIGN FIRM**
Paradowski Graphic Design
**DESIGNER**
Shawn Cornell

**ROCKY MOUNTAIN**

# COLLEGE
## OF ART +
# DESIGN

## ESPLANADE
*Place*

Rocky Mountain
ANGLERS ℠

# ENCOMPASS

CLIENT
Heartlab Cardiac Solutions
DESIGN FIRM
Malcolm Grear Designers

# FRIENDSHIP CLASSIC

## GULFPORT ROTARY GOLF TOURNAMENT

CLIENT
Rotary Club Of Gulfport
DESIGN FIRM
The Prime Time Group
DESIGNER
John Seymour

# GLOBAL FUND FOR WOMEN

CLIENT
Global Fund for Women
DESIGN FIRM
tompertdesign
DESIGNERS
Claudia Huber Tompert, Michael Tompert

cascades

CLIENT
Old Mutual Properties
DESIGN FIRM
Developement Design Group
DESIGNER
Bridget Parlato

TeraSolutions, Inc.

CLIENT
TeraSolutions, Inc.
DESIGN FIRM
Jeff Fisher LogoMotives
DESIGNER
Jeff Fisher

## BLACK BEAR
### GALLERY

CLIENT
   Black Bear Gallery
DESIGN FIRM
   Lomangino Studio Inc.
DESIGNER
   Kim Pollock

CLIENT
   Navegante Group-Tolstoy's Retail
DESIGN FIRM
   Ripple Strategic Design & Consulting
DESIGNERS
   Raymond Perez, Dan McElhattan II

CLIENT
   Vazza Properties
DESIGN FIRM
   Jasper & Bridge
DESIGNER
   Kim Noyes

CLIENT
   Grass Roots
DESIGN FIRM
   RG Design
DESIGNER
   Russ Garn

## VERACITY
### CAPITAL PARTNERS

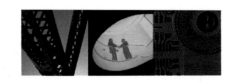

## VERACITY
### CAPITAL PARTNERS

## VERACITY
### CAPITAL PARTNERS

CLIENT
   Veracity Capital Partners
DESIGN FIRM
   Baker Designed Communications
DESIGNERS
   Brian Keenan, Michelle Wolins

# VARIAGENICS

*genes4life*

CLIENT
Variagenics Inc.
DESIGN FIRM
Gill Fishman Assoc.
DESIGNERS
Gill Fishman, Michael Persons

# NEWGROUND

CLIENT
NewGround Resources
DESIGN FIRM
Mortensen Design
DESIGNERS
PJ Niecker, Gordon Mortensen

# HORIZON™
## MECHANICAL, INC.

CLIENT
Horizon Mechanical Inc.
DESIGN FIRM
Genghis Design
DESIGNER
Dale Monahan

# D&R
## INTERNATIONAL

CLIENT
D&R International
DESIGN FIRM
Lazarus Design
DESIGNER
Robin Lazarus

# AMERICAN DSL
*Connecting The World.*
*At The Speed Of Your Imagination.*

CLIENT
American DSL
DESIGN FIRM
Michael Lee Advertising & Design
DESIGNERS
Michael Lee, Debby Stasinopoulou

CLIENT
Bell Dental Products, LLC
DESIGN FIRM
Mark Mock Design Assoc. Inc.
DESIGNER
James Chott

# BELL DENTAL

**CLIENT**
Divi Divi
**DESIGN FIRM**
Mike Salisbury
**DESIGNER**
Kristen Allen

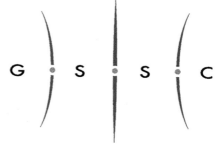

Consulting at the crossroads™

**CLIENT**
GSSC
**DESIGN FIRM**
Spark Design
**DESIGNER**
Joe Gunsten

SUPREMO

**CLIENT**
CreAgri
**DESIGN FIRM**
Mastandrea Design, Inc.
**DESIGNER**
MaryAnne Mastandrea

**CLIENT**
Stonewall Vineyard
**DESIGN FIRM**
Barbara Brown Marketing & Design
**DESIGNER**
Barbara Brown

Beverly
**Art**
Center

**CLIENT**
Beverly Art Center Logo
**DESIGN FIRM**
Crosby Associates Inc.
**DESIGNERS**
Bart Crosby, Malgorzata Sobus

VIGO COUNTY
HISTORICAL
*Society*

**CLIENT**
Vigo County Historical Society
**DESIGN FIRM**
Miller & White Advertising
**DESIGNER**
Lori Lucas

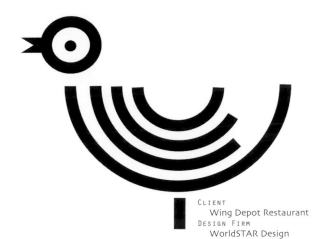

CLIENT
Wing Depot Restaurant
DESIGN FIRM
WorldSTAR Design
DESIGNER
Greg Guhl

CLIENT
BFF Hiking
DESIGN FIRM
WorldSTAR Design
DESIGNER
Greg Guhl

CLIENT
Ravel Housing Development
DESIGN FIRM
Greenhaus
DESIGNERS
Tracy Sabin, Craig Fuller

SOBER | SOBER P.C.

KEEPING YOUR BUSINESS ON TARGET

CLIENT
Sober & Sober P.C.
DESIGN FIRM
Pollman Marketing Arts, Inc.
DESIGNER
Jennifer Pollman

**1 0 1 0 1 0 1 0 4 0 1 0 1 0 1 0 1 0**
**1 0 1 0 1 0 1 0 4 0 1 0 1 0 1 0 1 0**

ITAA's 40TH MANAGEMENT CONFERENCE & CEO SUMMIT

**1 0 1 0 1 0 1 0 4 0 1 0 1 0 1 0 1 0**
**1 0 1 0 1 0 1 0 4 0 1 0 1 0 1 0 1 0**

CLIENT
Information Technology
Association of America
DESIGN FIRM
Lazarus Design
DESIGNER
Robin Lazarus

PERCEPTA™

CLIENT
Percepta
DESIGN FIRM
CommArts, Inc.
DESIGNERS
Richard Foy, Mark Jasin

CLIENT
20th Centry Fox
DESIGN FIRM
Mike Salisbury, LLC
DESIGNER
Leslie Carbaga

CLIENT
StockBridge Capital
DESIGN FIRM
WorkHorse Creative
DESIGNERS
David Vogin, Lesley Quesada

CLIENT
CreAgri, LLC
DESIGN FIRM
Mastandrea Design, Inc.
DESIGNER
Mary Anne Mastandrea

CLIENT
SkyRocketer
DESIGN FIRM
Kircher, Inc.
DESIGNER
Bruce E. Morgan

CLIENT
Sunny Hill Adventures
DESIGN FIRM
Fleishman-Hillard Design, St. Louis
DESIGNERS
John Senseney, Kevin Kampwerth

CLIENT
Nature Center at Shaker Lakes
DESIGN FIRM
Epstein Design Partners
DESIGNER
Gina Linehan

CLIENT
  Astaris
DESIGN FIRM
  Stan Gellman Graphic Design Inc.
DESIGNERS
  Mike Donovan, Barry Tilson

CLIENT
  WaddleSnout gifts
DESIGN FIRM
  TDH Marketing & Communications
DESIGNERS
  Donna Hull, Charles Moser III

CLIENT
  Ultimate Marketing
DESIGN FIRM
  The Wecker Group
DESIGNER
  Robert J. Wecker

CLIENT
  Spokane Parks Foundation
DESIGN FIRM
  Klundt Hosmer Design
DESIGNERS
  Darin Klundt, Amy Gunter
  Judy Heggem-Davis

CARNEGIE
MUSEUM OF ART
*One of the four Carnegie Museums of Pittsburgh*

CLIENT
  Carnegie Museum of Art
DESIGN FIRM
  Agnew Moyer Smith Inc.
DESIGNERS
  John Sotirakis, Gina Datres,
  Lisa Vitalbo, Jack Kelley

CLIENT
  Xelus
DESIGN FIRM
  McElveney & Palozzi Design Group, Inc.
DESIGNER
  Matt Nowicki

CLIENT
    Axcelera Specialty Risk
DESIGN FIRM
    De Martino Design
DESIGNER
    Erick De Martino

CLIENT
    Church of Hope
DESIGN FIRM
    Inklings Design + Associates
DESIGNERS
    J. Gruber, William Butler

CLIENT
    Future Kids
DESIGN FIRM
    Zamboo
DESIGNER
    Becca Bootes

CLIENT
    RidethePipe.com
DESIGN FIRM
    Gold & Associates
DESIGNERS
    Keith Gold, Peter Butcavage

CLIENT
    CRE8IVE, LLC
DESIGN FIRM
    Visual Marketing Associates, Inc.
DESIGNERS
    Jen Dutcher, Al Hidalgo

CLIENT
    Near Space
DESIGN FIRM
    The Marketing Store
DESIGNER
    Calvina Yang Ngnyen

# workhorse>

CLIENT
Workhorse Technologies
DESIGN FIRM
Agnew Moyer Smith Inc.
DESIGNER
John Sotirakis

CLIENT
Bluearc
DESIGN FIRM
Michael Patrick Partners
DESIGNERS
Mike Mescall, Connie Hwang,
Stephanie West, Jenny Herrick

CLIENT
Straight Away
DESIGN FIRM
Frankfurt Balkind Partners
DESIGNER
David Suh

CLIENT
Ejasent
DESIGN FIRM
Anvil Graphic Design
DESIGNERS
Lori Rosales, Laura Bauer

CLIENT
Association of Government Accountants
DESIGN FIRM
TGD Communications
DESIGNERS
Chris Harrison, Jennifer Cedoz,
Rochelle Gray

CLIENT
Planet Cargo
DESIGN FIRM
Baer Design Group
DESIGNER
Todd Baer

CLIENT
Tango Cat
DESIGN FIRM
Paradowski Graphic Design
DESIGNER
Shawn Cornell

CLIENT
AppraisalHub.com
DESIGN FIRM
Extraprise Group, Inc.
DESIGNERS
Andy Harding, Julie Tsuchiya,
Mark Sloneker

**VoiceSignal**

CLIENT
Voice Signal
DESIGN FIRM
Gill Fishman Assoc.
DESIGNER
Michael Persons, Gill Fishman

virtualteams.com

CLIENT
Virtual Teams/Net Age
DESIGN FIRM
Gill Fishman Assoc.
DESIGNERS
Gill Fishman, Alicia Ozyjowski

CLIENT
Salsaritas Fresh Burrito
DESIGN FIRM
Shook
DESIGNERS
Jeff Camillo, Ginger Riley

**Design Central**

CLIENT
Design Central
DESIGN FIRM
Design Central
DESIGNERS
Daniel Kidwell, Gregg Davis,
Rudiger Joppe

**CLIENT**
Reston Town Center Association
**DESIGN FIRM**
Grasp Creative, Inc.
**DESIGNER**
Doug Fuller

**CLIENT**
Random Walk Computing
**DESIGN FIRM**
Cullinane Design Inc.
**DESIGNER**
Carmen Li

**CLIENT**
Vertel Corporation
**DESIGN FIRM**
The Artime Group
**DESIGNERS**
Lisa Sarkissian, Henry Artime,
Nuria Romero

**CLIENT**
Stern Marketing Group
**DESIGN FIRM**
Mortensen Design
**DESIGNERS**
PJ Nidecker, Gordon Mortensen,
Wendy Chon

**CLIENT**
HCIA Sachs
**DESIGN FIRM**
McKnight Kurland Baccelli

**CLIENT**
Meridian Technologies
**DESIGN FIRM**
Empire Communications Group
**DESIGNER**
Phil Helow

CLIENT
Inter•Continental Hotels & Resorts
DESIGN FIRM
Degnen Associates, Inc.
DESIGNERS
Dave Fowler, Steve Degnen

CLIENT
Breakaway Solutions
DESIGN FIRM
Cipriani Kremer Design
DESIGNER
Robert Cipriani

CLIENT
Lee & Hayes, PLLC
DESIGN FIRM
Klundt Hosmer Design
DESIGNER
Darin Klundt

METROPOLITAN

Metropolitan Achievement Test     Eighth Edition

CLIENT
Harcourt Brace Educational Measurement
DESIGN FIRM
Smarteam Communications, Inc.
DESIGNERS
Gary Ridley, Lisa Carey

E · LOGICITY

CLIENT
elogicity
DESIGN FIRM
Twist
DESIGNER
Chris Rossi

Spa for the Spirit

CLIENT
Spa for the Spirit
DESIGN FIRM
Rassman Design
DESIGNERS
John Rassman, Amy Rassman

# Designers

## Clients

### Symbols

317